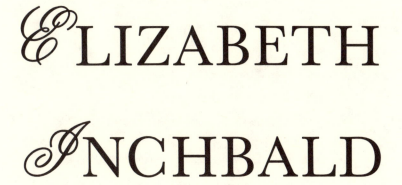

ELIZABETH

INCHBALD

*England's Principal Woman Dramatist
and Independent Woman of Letters in
18th Century London*

A BIOGRAPHICAL STUDY

ROGER MANVELL

Author of
SARAH SIDDONS *and* ELLEN TERRY

UNIVERSITY
PRESS OF
AMERICA

Lanham • New York • London

Copyright © 1987 by

University Press of America,® Inc.

4720 Boston Way
Lanham, MD 20706

3 Henrietta Street
London WC2E 8LU England

British Cataloging in Publication Information Available

Library of Congress Cataloging-in-Publication Data

Manvell, Roger, 1909-
Elizabeth Inchbald : England's principal woman
dramatist and independent woman of letters in 18th
century London.

Bibliography: p.
Includes index.
1. Inchbald, Mrs., 1753-1821.   2. Authors, English—
18th century—Biography.   3. Actors—England—
Biography.   I. Title.
PR3518.Z5M36 1987   822'.4 [B]   87-21247
ISBN 0-8191-6633-2 (alk. paper)
ISBN 0-8191-6634-0 (pbk. : alk. paper)

To

Françoise

iii

ENGRAVED BY HEATH FROM AN ORIGINAL PICTURE.
PUBLISH'D BY LONGMAN AND CO
1806

Elizabeth Inchbald
Portrait (1806) as published in
<u>The British Theatre</u>

CONTENTS

This is the first full-scale biography of Elizabeth Inchbald since that published in 1833 by James Boaden. S.R. Littlewood's Elizabeth Inchbald and her Circle (1921) is brief, somewhat slight, and entirely derived from Boaden. Critical study of her work, either as dramatist or as novelist (though with little or no detailed biographical content for its own sake) has been much more serious, notably in the case of Gary Kelly's The English Jacobin Novel 1780-1805 (1976) and two unpublished theses, William McKee's Elizabeth Inchbald: Novelist (1935) and Bruce Robertson Park's Thomas Holcroft and Elizabeth Inchbald: Studies in the 18th Century Drama of Ideas (1952). There is also the thesis, The Life and Work of Mrs. Inchbald, undertaken during the 1930s and held at Harvard University, by G. Louis Joughin, to whom credit must also go for making a thorough bibliographical listing of her work, to which should be added the authoritative listing of the plays only given by Allardyce Nicoll in Vol. III of his A History of the English Drama 1660-1900: Late Eighteenth Century Drama. To all these I am indebted.

It is deplorable that the writer who should rank as Britain's principal woman dramatist should not in 1987 have a single one of her twenty-one plays available in popularly accessible editions (as distinct from certain extremely expensive facsimile editions), in spite of the opinion of her contemporary, John Genest - 'She was little inferior to any of her contemporaries, and very superior to most of them' - and of Allardyce Nicoll, who refers to the 'brilliance' and the 'brightness' of her dialogue, and her work in general as 'fresh, honest and thoughtful' and at its best worthy to stand alongside that of Sheridan. Even the least of her plays makes entertaining and interesting reading. It is true that Aphra Behn (1640-89) had preceded her over a century earlier as a celebrated woman dramatist - she wrote fifteen plays between 1671 and 1689 - but her success lay in her capacity to write comedies of intrigue like her male contemporaries, while her fame is to a considerable extent based on her adventurous life and capacity to hold her own in the male-dominated society of the Restoration theatre. Of Elizabeth Inchbald's two novels, Nature and Art has been out of print for a century. Only A Simple Story, her principal novel, exists in modern editions. It is for this reason I have been generous in introducing quotations, so that the quality of her writing, both as novelist and dramatist, can begin to be adequately assessed.

I have been assisted generously during the course of preparing this biographical and critical study. In America I owe much to the help and support given me by Vice President Gerald Gross of Boston University, and by Mr. John P. Laucus, Librarian of Boston University, and his staff. I am also grateful to the staff of the libraries at Harvard University and the Folger Shakespeare Library. In England I have always received great help from the Librarian and staff at London University, and I also owe thanks to the staff at Dartmouth Library in Devon. I want to thank Jennifer Aylmer, formerly Curator of the British Theatre Museum before and after it was rehoused at the Victoria and Albert Museum in London, where some material relevant to Elizabeth Inchbald is held, and also the Manuscript Department of the British Museum. I have received much practical support from my own College at Boston University - the College of Communication - during the months of preparation of the typescript, and especially from Ms. Phyllis Robbins, who prepared the camera-ready script. Finally, I would like to thank my wife, Françoise, for her constant help and support, and Ms. Helen Hudson of the University Press of America, who advised on and supervised the book production.

ROGER MANVELL

Dartmouth, Devon, England
Boston University, Boston, Massachusetts, USA

John Philip Kemble as Coriolanus
Portrait by Sir Thomas Lawrence
(Victoria and Albert Museum, London)

I

ACTRESS

Anyone joining the East Anglian express coach to London, known as the Norwich Fly, on 11 April 1772, would have seen as a fellow traveler a young girl of eighteen, alone without companion or chaperone. This, the casual observer might have thought, was unusual for a girl of her age. No one could have overlooked her unless he were blind, for Elizabeth Simpson was of exceptional beauty; one who knew her well described her somewhat later as 'tall, slender, straight, of the purest complexion ... her hair of golden auburn, her eyes full at once of spirit and sweetness.'[1] Now, however, she was very tense. A country girl, a farmer's daughter, she was setting out with a firm intent to make her own way in the world, to be independent of her provincial family. And this, she believed, she could only achieve in London.

It was, of course, a risky business. London and its suburbs in the last third of the eighteenth century had a population of some three quarters of a million — when England and Wales together composed only some seven and a half million. Although the capital represented a great and vigorous center of culture, it was also a violent and dangerous place. Rapidly expanding, its built-up areas extended by now west to Tiburn Lane (now Park Lane) and Hyde Park. Buckingham House had only ten years before become a royal residence with a country setting to the west, though just to the east lay the buildings surrounding Whitehall and Westminster, still a relatively isolated district. Tiburn Road (the present Oxford Street) leading to the much shorter Oxford Street of the time had dwellings extending north along Portland Street and fringing here and there Tottenham Court Road, while further east, north of High Holborn, residences extended only just beyond Bloomsbury Square and Great Ormond Street. To the east the fields began to show green at Whitechapel Street and beyond Smithfield. To the south, Bermondsey was still open country, while Mile End was a little

country town. South of the river urban development
was soon absorbed into countryside, the major
development being opposite St. Paul's Cathedral and
south of London Bridge. Blackfriar's Bridge had
been opened recently in 1769, while the houses
crossing old London Bridge over the river itself
had been pulled down only eighteen years previously.

The heart of old London remained what is
called the City; Dr. Samuel Johnson's London
centered on Fleet Street and the Inner Temple, a
brief stroll from St. Paul's, while the royal
patent theatres of Drury Lane (of which David
Garrick had become manager in 1747) and Covent
Garden were barely ten minutes' walk away. But for
a young woman on her own the crowded, often narrow
streets and alley ways of London were a hazard, and
women who had a care for their safety or their
reputation were usually accompanied by their
menfolk, other mature women, or their servants, at
least when they ventured abroad in the city.

The Norwich Fly reached London - a distance
of only some 40 miles from Elizabeth's home in
Suffolk - and put down its passengers. She
collected her baggage and sought refuge from the
crowds as quickly as she could in a tavern, the
Rose and Crown in St. John's Street, situated in
central London. Elizabeth has left no record of
how she slept that night. But she knew what she
was about; she had a plan of campaign. Although
she had several close relatives in London, at this
stage she only wanted to avoid them. After all,
she had just run away from home. She remained
determined not to make contact with her London
relatives. She walked later in the day to Covent
Garden, always fearful she would catch sight of one
or other of her kin. She was determined to seek
out on her own initiative the key theatrical
manager of the day, Thomas King of Drury Lane, but
she failed at this early stage to secure the
interview she sought. For her objective, which she
knew her relatives would endeavor to thwart, was to
become an actress, however humbly placed in the
London theatre. But by now, everything seemed to
threaten her, and the London she desired to accept
her, to have become nothing but an alien and
dangerous haunt. She was afraid of her landlady,
and moved her lodging to the White Swan on Holborn
Bridge (near present-day Holborn Circus) where, she

said later, she was held in great suspicion, though she pretended to be a passenger unable to obtain a place on a coach just leaving for York. The hostess, she said, locked her in her attic bedroom where, since she had little money, she subsisted on bread and water.[2]

On 15 April, five days after her arrival in London, she managed to make at last some positive contact with Thomas King. She gave him her name - Elizabeth Simpson - but nothing came of this interview, if such it was. She had spent her spare time, of which she had had only too much, not only walking in London (excursions undertaken in part to deceive the hostess at the inn that she was visiting friends) but also studying plays including Othello and The Tempest - for she fancied herself as both Desdemona and Miranda. But she was forced to accept that she could no longer hold out without the help of her elder sisters, no less than four of whom were married and lived in London; she knew that she was risking their disfavor and insistence that she return to her mother's house in Suffolk. So on 16 April she posted a letter to her sister, Dorothy Hunt. Then she had to wait until 20 April for contact to be made.[3]

The home she had left so precipitately appears to have been a comfortable and contented one. Elizabeth was not escaping from a tyrannous existence. She was a member of what appears to have been a numerous and united family. Born on 15 October 1753 at Standingfield (now Stanningfield) near Bury St. Edmunds in Suffolk, she was one of John and Mary Simpson's many daughters. They owned what her near-contemporary biographer, James Boaden, an addict of theatre history and enthusiastic friend of many of the great personalities of the eighteenth-century theatre, called a 'moderate farm.' The Simpsons were Catholics, but Boaden says were nevertheless 'greatly esteemed' by the gentry of the neighborhood. Elizabeth's father had died in 1761 when she was only seven years old, and this had put some strain on the family income, for there were in all two sons, George and Edward, and six daughters, including Anne, Dorothy, and Deborah. By 1770 four of the girls had married, and had left with their husbands for London. Anne and Dorothy had married two brothers, John and James Hunt; two of the other girls married a Mr. Huggins and a Mr. Slender, whose name at least had a pleasant link with Shakespeare. Edward had also married and lived nearby. Deborah and Elizabeth had remained for the time being at home.

Although George went to school for seven years (and, says his sister, 'never could spell'), Elizabeth and two of her sisters had no formal schooling, but could (she claims) 'spell from our infancy.' Elizabeth's education was therefore 'domestic,' as was the case for many middle-class girls in the 1760s and 1770s. 'Though she shunned company,' writes Boaden, 'she longed to see the world. The Metropolis, in fact, became her passion.' London was her objective - 'to London she would bend her course.' Even at so early an age as 13, she had declared 'she would rather die, than live any longer without seeing the world.'[4]

Not that Standingfield was an over-remote village. It was situated about six miles south of Bury St. Edmunds, or St. Edmunds Bury as Daniel Defoe termed it in his A Tour thro' the Whole Island of Great Britain, published in 1724, some thirty years before Elizabeth was born. He described Bury as 'the Montpelier of Suffolk ... famed for its pleasant situation and wholesome air ... in proportion to its bigness, most thronged with gentry, people of the best fashion, the most polite conversation ... the ladies mighty gay and agreeable.' He went on to say that 'at the time of the fair in this town ... one hardly sees such a show in any part of the world,' with 'assemblies' every night. Some forty miles north of Bury stood Norwich, capital of Norfolk, one of the most populated areas of Britain; as Defoe wrote, '120,000 people [were] employed in the woollen and silk and wool manufactures of that city,' though the employees included children of four and five years working at home, as many did. Norwich, with city walls three miles in circumference, had a fine cathedral, and was 'ancient, large, rich and populous.' Like Bury, it also boasted a theatre.[5]

Elizabeth had developed her love for the theater at a very early age. Her ambition was to become an actress, but there was one impediment. She stammered. This made her shy; she 'shunned company,' says Boaden, though her home had many visitors. She set out determinedly to cope with her defect. According to Boaden, 'she wrote out all the words with which she had much difficulty; carried them constantly about her; and moreover discovered that stage declamation, being a raised and artificial thing, afforded more time for enunciation.' In other words, she stammered more in the haste of ordinary conversation than she did when declaiming theatrical speech, which she constantly set herself the task of rehearsing and performing. Not only was she an assiduous student of literature, she studied and recited the texts of plays. The family loved reading aloud and having play recitals, and whenever she could, Elizabeth went with members of the family to the theatres of Norwich and Bury.

Early in 1770, when she was only sixteen, she wrote in secret to Richard Griffith, manager of the theatre in Norwich, asking boldly for an engagement. He replied courteously inviting her to come and see him, though making it clear he had no place to offer her in his company. It seems that she had developed a girlish 'crush' on the actor, for in her private diary (which she preserved, and which Boaden saw) she spelled out his name in capitals, RICHARD GRIFFITH, and added, 'Each dear letter of thy name is harmony.' Her strong feeling for him was to last some while.

In Bury, which served as the post-town to which their mail was delivered, they came to know the players in the theatre, and Elizabeth's brother George, who was also stage-struck, became an actor in the Bury company in April 1770. This enabled her when visiting Bury (where some family cousins lived) to attend rehearsals. She began to copy out parts that she favored, such as Shakespeare's Hermione and Cordelia. One of the actors in Bury, Mr. Wilson, was among her earliest admirers, and was later to prove helpful to her. She was to be peculiarly susceptible to admiration from men - and this was to cause many difficulties for her in the future.

In May 1771, when she was 17, Elizabeth was able to make her first visit to London, now that her four married sisters lived there. She stayed with Dorothy Hunt, who lived in Orange Street, near Leicester Square. Now at last she could see the sights, enjoy London company, and above all go to the theatre. She stayed until 4 June. Among the people she met was the actor and painter, Joseph Inchbald, who was 36. It would appear that he immediately fell in love with her, and she was no doubt at least attracted to him (or to his profession), although she came to realize fairly soon that he had had connections in the past, since he had two sons, George, who was also an actor, and Bob, who was still a child. As no mention is ever made of any previous marriage for Joseph Inchbald, it would seem that both sons were illegitimate. Just before Joseph left London to undertake a professional engagement in Birmingham and she was due to return to Standingfield, they went together to Vauxhall Gardens across the river as members of a party. Vauxhall had shady walks where nightingales sang, and was a great center in London for banqueting and music; like Ranelagh Gardens, situated in what is now Chelsea, Vauxhall was a fashionable resort of the gentry for eating and drinking, with promenades and, in the case of Ranelagh, a Rotunda 150 feet in diameter, making up an amphitheatre with 48 boxes, painted and gilded, and space for an orchestra. It was lit by chandeliers holding candles set in crystal glass. Vauxhall had a thousand lamps which were timed to illuminate together, making a sudden, unique and astonishing blaze of light.

The splendors of London excited Elizabeth to make fresh efforts to become an actress. Accompanied by her sister, Mrs. Slender, she went to Norwich to try to speak with Richard Griffith, though she actually did not meet him until 15 June, not in Norwich, but at Bury where she was attending the annual fair and staying for a week with her cousin. Her attachment to Richard Griffith continued; she recorded in the diary she allowed Boaden to see:

1772. Jan 22. Saw Mr. Griffith's picture.
      Jan 28. Stole it.

Nevertheless she added on January 29: 'Rather disappointed at not receiving a letter from Mr. Inchbald.'[6]

He, poor man, had been pressing his suit with both Elizabeth and her mother since the previous

June, and apparently correspondence had continued, with gaps, throughout the rest of 1771. Boaden reproduces Elizabeth's heavily self-conscious reply to one of his more serious letters:

> You see, Mr. Inchbald, I have complied with your request, by answering your letter immediately. Indeed, I was not a little disturbed at first sight of it, with wondering what new correspondent I had got; for as so many things of consequence had occurred since I saw the hand, it had already slipt my remembrance ... I find you have seen my thoughts on marriage; but, as you desire it, I will repeat them. In spite of your eloquent pen, matrimony still appears to me with less charms than terrors: the bliss arising from it, I doubt not, is superior to any other - but best not to be ventured for (in my opinion), till some little time have proved the emptiness of all other; which it seldom fails to do. But to enter into marriage with the least reluctance, as fearing you are going to sacrifice part of your time, must be greatly imprudent: fewer unhappy matches I think would be occasioned, if fewer persons were guilty of this indiscretion, - an indiscretion that shocks me, and which I hope Heaven will ever preserve me from; as must be your wish, if the regard that you have professed for me be really mine, which I am not wholly undeserving of; for, as much as the strongest friendship can allow, I am, yours, E. Simpson.[7]

Though it is plain that, at the age of 17, she did not want to tie herself to this man in his middle thirties, she did not want entirely to choke him off. She knew he could be useful to her. By now she was seriously contemplating running off on her own to London since Richard Griffith was still unable to do anything for her. She had confided her local ambitions to both George and to Dorothy Hunt. She determined to make one more effort in Norwich, and went there secretly by coach. But it still did no good. So, thwarted in this direction, she packed up her few belongings and left home in secret to catch the Norwich Fly to London. She left another, rather melodramatic and self-conscious letter of farewell for her mother:

> By the time you receive this I shall have left Standingfield, and perhaps for ever. You are surprised, but be not uneasy:- believe the step I have taken, however indiscreet, is no ways criminal; unless I sin by not acquainting you with it, which was impossible for me to do, though strongly pressed by the desire of giving you a personal farewell. I now endure every pang - one not lost to all feeling must - on thus quitting the tenderest and best of parents; I would say most beloved too, but cannot <u>prove</u> my affection;- yet time may;- to <u>that</u> I must submit my hope of regaining your regard. The censure of the world I despise; as the most worthy incur the reproaches of <u>that</u>. Should I ever think you wish to hear from me, I will write.[8]

*   *   *   *

The 1770s in London was an interesting decade. Much had happened or was to happen. The 1770s were to see Johnson, now in his sixties, touring the Hebrides with Boswell (whom he had met for the first time in 1763, when Boswell was only 22), and then follow up this tour by visits to both Wales and France with his friends, Henry and Hester Thrale, as well as writing his <u>Lives of the Poets</u>. While the decade saw the deaths of Goldsmith, Smollett and Garrick, it included also the births of William Wordsworth, Samuel Taylor Coleridge, Charles Lamb, William Hazlitt, and Walter Scott. There was also the publication of the first edition of the Encyclopaedia Britannica, of Smollett's <u>Humphrey Clinker</u>, of Fanny Burney's <u>Evelina</u>, and the first performances of Goldsmith's <u>She Stoops to Conquer</u>, and of Sheridan's <u>The Rivals</u> and <u>The School for Scandal</u>. Between 1750 and 1800 the sale of books in Britain increased by ten times, and circulating libraries flourished. Critical reviews began to be published; the sale of journals doubled between 1750 and 1775, though the total sale of newspapers as such in Britain during the year 1774 was only 12,300,000. The figure was to increase to 14 million by 1790.[9] Thomas Gainsborough and Sir Joshua Reynolds (recently knighted in 1769) were at the height of their fame as portrait painters, and John Constable, painter of a future era, was born. Abroad, Britain was suffering a succession of defeats in the struggle to retain possession of the American colonies. In neighboring France, the Encyclopédie, the epitome of anti-conservative, rational, deist, scientific, materialistic, and humanistic thinking of the period, had been completed and indexed by 1780 in 35 volumes, edited by Denis Diderot, and with contributions from writers such as Rousseau and Voltaire.

In the British theatre, Elizabeth's contemporary, and future friend, Sarah Siddons (England's greatest actress in the 18th century) was during the 1770s to make her name as an actress the hard way in the flourishing theatres of the English provinces, as well as in Scotland and Ireland, though she failed on her initial appearance in London during Garrick's final season at Drury Lane in 1775-76. In 1775 her brother, John Philip Kemble, later to become Elizabeth's closest male friend, finally abandoned his studies for the priesthood at Douai in France, and joined his sister to become eventually England's greatest actor after the death of Garrick.

The theatres in 18th century London were led by the two that enjoyed the privilege of holding the royal patent, Drury Lane and Covent Garden. The licensing of theatres had been introduced over a century before in 1660 by Charles II in order to exercise a close political control over what was presented on the stage. The chosen licensed theatres in London and the provinces were known as Theatres Royal, receiving their license from the Lord Chamberlain, an official of the King's household, whose office was also responsible for perusing and licensing every new play performed, a responsibility to survive until the abolition of theatre censorship in Britain in 1968. This led to the use of the terms 'legitimate' and 'illegitimate' in connection with the theatre. Companies working in unlicensed theatres or centers of performance either in London or the provinces could only charge admission for musical presentations; plays as such (if offered at all) appeared nominally free of charge, a bonus for audiences and an outlet for actors hungry to qualify for engagements in 'legitimate' drama. Since there were no theatre schools or recognized forms of training in acting other than being accepted in some humble position or other in the performing companies spread all through the provinces, aspiring actors and actresses could do nothing but plead to be accepted into a company and allowed to learn their craft by appearing with and observing the techniques of the experienced. They began by 'walking on,' and graduated by undertaking small supporting roles which in the course of time, if they showed promise, became more prominent. This was the position in which Elizabeth found herself in London; still undaunted, she continued in her attempts to secure interviews with the managers or their associates at the principal London theatres, although the usual method of entering the theatre was to join a modestly established company in the provinces.

It was on April 20 that Elizabeth met the most sympathetic of her married sisters, Dorothy Hunt, taking tea with her in her garden. It appears this meeting did not result in any major trouble. In fact, she appears to have been readily accepted by all her sisters in London.

Elizabeth moved that same day to stay with another of her married sisters, Mrs. Huggins. On 22 May she met Joseph Inchbald again, and the following month was reconciled without much trouble with her mother by correspondence. She visited the theatre not less than twice a week, and began again to try out the possibilities of getting an engagement at one or other of the London playhouses. An actor-manager, James Dodd, seemed ready to engage her, but tried to exact in return the privilege also of seducing her. She had a number of meetings with him between 18 and 22 May, and records that she was at first 'rather frighted' and then later 'terrified and vexed beyond measure at his behaviour,' so much so that she threw a basin of hot water in his face.[10] Further interviews with Richard Griffith (presumably in London) still led to nothing, but by now Inchbald was pressing his suit upon her and seeing her daily. On 9 June 1772 she was married to him by a

Catholic priest - Inchbald was also a Catholic, another point of contact between them - and on 10 June after breakfast at the Slenders' house, they were married again according to Protestant rites.[11] On 11 June they set off by coach for Bristol where Inchbald was engaged to play Lear on 29 June, though by the 27th he proved to be too ill to do so.

The marriage of Elizabeth and Joseph might well be considered to have been one of convenience. While there is little doubt he was sexually ensnared by her beauty, and had been in love with her ever since he had first set eyes on her a year before, there were probably mixed motives for the marriage on her side. She had learned that there was little likelihood she would get a theatrical engagement on her own, especially with her speech impediment. Obsessed with the stage and impetuous in her desire to become an actress, she needed small encouragement to marry into the theatre. Inchbald was a competent and well-established performer; though by no means a great actor, he was reliable and more in work than out of it, playing leading parts in London as well as in the provinces. His health however was indifferent, as Elizabeth was soon enough to learn, having to nurse him two weeks after their marriage during what should have been a honeymoon period. Although still uninvited to try her capacity on the stage, she occupied her time writing voluminously to her mother, her sisters, and her actor-brother, George. But being married now to a leading actor, she determined to win through, and she was permitted to appear as Cordelia (the part she had learned and re-learned, copied out and re-copied) to her husband's Lear on 4 September 1772. He insisted on hearing her speak her lines; according to Boaden, 'they spouted (as she plainly calls it) at home and in the open air, till at length she hit upon a better tone of declamation than she had set out with.' Boaden does not think she made much impression on her first audiences, but it was a start. By 18 September her husband's engagement was finished, and the couple returned to London. On the whole they seem to have enjoyed themselves, having on off days managed to visit nearby Wales, as well as Bath and Weston; on their return to London they visited Elizabeth's mother in Standingfield before leaving on 10 October by sea

11

for Scotland to join West Digges's company and perform in Glasgow and Edinburgh.

They were to remain in Digges's company until 1776, acting throughout Scotland, primarily in Edinburgh and Glasgow, but working on occasion also in Greenock, Aberdeen, Dundee and Dumfries. During these three and a half years, and the succeeding short seasons with Joseph Younger's and Tate Wilkinson's managements, Elizabeth built up her repertoire of parts, playing principals in over thirty different plays, as well as many small parts, including that of one of the witches in Macbeth. These principal roles included many in Shakespeare (Cordelia, Anne Bullen, Lady Anne, Lady Percy, Desdemona, Miranda, Juliet, and Imogen), Cleopatra in Dryden's All for Love, several of Rowe's heroines (Calista in The Fair Penitent, Aspasia in Tamerlane, and the title role in Jane Shore), Belvidera in Otway's Venice Preserved, Miss Neville in Goldsmith's She Stoops to Conquer and Lady Sneerwell in Sheridan's The School for Scandal.

The Inchbalds had to endure a hard life of constant travel, often under the most trying of conditions, living in inns and lodgings, studying new roles - though since both of them were earning the very modest wages of provincial players, a time largely without severe financial worry. They were to have no children, but Bob Inchbald, still a boy, reappeared from time to time to rejoin his father (and occasionally was the cause of dissension between them), while George Inchbald, Joseph's older son, was working independently as an actor and now and then joined the same company. Elizabeth, too, kept in touch with her numerous relatives, and seldom missed an opportunity when they went south to visit Standingfield.

The marriage, however, could scarcely be called a success, and Boaden, who as a biographer always prefers to look on the bright side, does not in this case try to hide the differences that constantly arose. Elizabeth's sharp tongue and sharper temper, and Inchbald's inability to control his jealousy when younger and more lively men than he tried to attract the attention of his youthful and beautiful wife led to most of the trouble between them. During the greater period of their marriage, before Inchbald's sudden death in 1779,

12

Elizabeth was in her early twenties, while he was in his late thirties and early forties. She was excited that her great gamble had come off and that she had been accepted as a competent actress entrusted by such established managers as Digges and the even more celebrated Tate Wilkinson with leading parts in Shakespeare, Rowe and the dramatists of the day. And she was undoubtedly responsive to the flattering attentions of certain of the men who courted her, they without doubt believing that so young and attractive a girl who had taken to the stage would also take to them in preference to her 'elderly' husband.

So their domestic quarrels started early. By the time they had reached Scotland, Boaden mentions the 'too frequent disputes between her husband and herself,' suggesting that Inchbald was in the habit of going out together with the actor, Richard Wilson, who was living in the same lodgings, and leaving her alone with young Bob Inchbald who, it seems, she did not much like. Her husband's actor friend was the same Richard Wilson who had paid her particular attention when he was a member of the company at Bury; he was, says Boaden coyly, 'never very regular in his habits.' Later another actor in the Scottish company, a Mr. Sterling (who played Iago to Inchbald's Othello and her Desdemona) was 'engaging the esteem of this beautiful woman,' carefully timing his visits to coincide with her husband's frequent absences. Elizabeth even resorted to her confessor in this case, and for a while forbade him her company, but saw fit fairly soon to relax her prohibitions. They would sit and read together, and when Inchbald accused his wife of 'apathy' she rounded on him and interpreted his absences as 'infidelity.' 'Her displeasure against Mr. Inchbald made her insist upon separate chambers more than once,' - this less than a year after their marriage. When professional engagements separated her from Sterling she carried on correspondence with him and, notes Boaden, 'discontinued her visits to chapel.' Inchbald persisted in absenting himself with his crony, Wilson, and was ill received when he came home drunk. Elizabeth let Sterling renew his visits when she and her husband returned to the main company in Edinburgh. However, Boaden always implies reconciliation between husband and wife, insisting on 'his affectionate and hearted value for

13

her,' and Joseph nursed her assiduously when, in September 1773, she was seriously ill with ague and fever. Her physician, Dr. Brodie, was later to form an attachment with her. When she was better, Inchbald took her for walks and read to her while she sat and worked, and she in turn became more reconciled to the presence of her stepson, Bob, with whom she played at cards. But she angered her husband afresh in Dumfries, where he was acting as temporary manager, by suddenly cutting off her hair for no stated reason.

So if it was not one thing it was another. In February, says Boaden, 'her husband and she disputed concerning <u>parting of salary</u>.'[12] It must not be forgotten that a wife's earnings were by law entirely at her husband's disposal, and without doubt (as her later novels bear out) she was highly aware of this affront to her sense of independence. By mid-year Sterling's attentions had grown less assiduous, but his place was to be taken later by a Mr. Webb, who called not once but sometimes twice a day, and in consequence the rows between husband and wife resumed. After recording that she was often reduced to tears, Boaden, in an effort to patch things up, biographically speaking, adds that Inchbald, 'with a few foibles' appears to have been 'a remarkably attentive and domestic husband.'[13]

By now she was 22, and soon to meet the man who was to mean more to her as a friend than any other. Her social life was normally lively. She and Inchbald were, apart from minor differences, friendly with their manager, West Digges, and the actress who lived with him, Miss Waterson; sometimes they even lodged alongside in the same premises. Mostly Elizabeth's associates were other players in the company, but socially speaking players were not 'gentry,' and no doubt she missed the kind of gentlefolk with whom she had been used to associate in Suffolk.

The termination of their long engagement with Digges in July 1776 followed what Boaden terms a dispute between Inchbald and his audience - an incident not uncommon in the 18th century theatre, when audiences were vociferous if displeased with a player, who if he were spirited enough would often answer back from the stage. The matter became sufficiently serious for the Inchbalds to decide to quit Edinburgh; and they had adequate savings and felt they owed themselves a vacation. Inchbald, disillusioned, wanted to develop what he always regarded as his second profession - painting, especially of miniatures. Elizabeth had been studying French with her usual assiduity since January of the previous year because she believed this necessary for her second profession. She was already developing her ambition to become a writer. What could be better, therefore, but to spend some time in France?- for Britain was not at this time engaged in any form of hostilities with her Continental neighbor. So they took ship from Shields in Scotland on 7 July 1776 and after two weeks' passage reached St. Valéry on 23 July. Once in France, they enjoyed living openly as Catholics, attending Mass in Abbeville. They arrived in Paris via Amiens on 23 July. Once there, they were befriended by an Abbé who showed them the sights of the capital. They also made friends with a Friar Jerningham, who was later to give Elizabeth advice when she underwent a period of religious doubt. Inchbald apparently took lessons in painting, while Elizabeth studied the technique of declamation in the French theatres. But their visit was not to last long; a letter from Elizabeth's mother in Standingfield made it clear they could expect no financial help from home. Their money was fast running out; they left Paris for Dieppe, where they stayed about three weeks while Elizabeth set about writing a farce. By the time they had crossed the Channel to Brighton they were so low in funds Boaden repeats the celebrated story that on one occasion they were forced to eat raw turnips they found in a field.[14] There was no immediate work for them either in Brighton or London, but finally they secured engagements on 11 October with Joseph Younger's company in Liverpool.

But undoubtedly the most important social event in Elizabeth's period on tour was her meeting with Sarah Siddons and her husband. A lifelong friendship was to develop between the two women, and later between Elizabeth and Sarah's younger brother, John Philip Kemble, who was to become England's greatest actor-manager in the latter part of the century. The Siddons and the Inchbalds met in 1776 in Liverpool, both couples working for Joseph Younger, who had engaged Sarah, at that time

aged 23, and in the process of rebuilding her
reputation in the provincial theatre after her
disastrous season with Garrick in London in
1775-76.[15] She was eight months younger than
Elizabeth, but she had been on the stage since
childhood. She was the daughter of the provincial
actor-manager, Roger Kemble, and was therefore far
more experienced in the ways of the theatre, and of
Drury Lane in particular.

In Liverpool and Manchester[16] the Siddons and
the Inchbalds and (later) Kemble were much together
socially (apart from short breaks) from mid-October
1776 until June 1777. Sarah introduced her brother
to Elizabeth in Manchester on 18 January.
Elizabeth was then 23 years old and John Philip two
weeks short of 20. Boaden, who was to be
biographer to Kemble as well as to Elizabeth,
describes him: 'his countenance remarkably
striking, his figure, though muscular, slender.'
He adds that,

> he greatly exceeded the usual
> measure of learning among young men, was
> very domestic in his habits, and fond of
> a friendly fireside, where he could read
> aloud if it was desired, or take his
> share in any sports, however trivial, or
> any occupations, however slight.

Elizabeth, susceptible as ever, responded.
According to Boaden,

> She seems to have paid him the
> homage of very particular study as a
> character out of the common road, and
> consequently in some danger of losing
> his way; for as to the powers of his
> genius, perhaps they needed the
> brilliant success of his sister to warm
> them to their full expansion, and
> prepare the public for a style of acting
> somewhat scholastic and systematic.[17]

Inchbald of course grew jealous again as
Kemble increased his visits. Nevertheless, towards
the end of March a joint excursion was planned
involving the Siddons, the Inchbalds, Kemble and
some other actors. They journeyed out to the moors
by chaise. 'While her husband paints,' writes

Boaden, 'Mrs. Inchbald reads with Mr. Kemble. In the afternoon they all walk out, and in the evening play cards, and sometimes get more infantine in their sports: these clever people go out upon the moor to play at "blindman's buff" or "puss in the corner".' Later, on Sundays, Boaden records that the Inchbalds read the Mass together in French out loud to Kemble. When they all moved from Manchester to Birmingham, Kemble rode in a post-chaise with the ladies, while Inchbald rode horseback. It was Kemble now, not Inchbald, who heard Elizabeth her lines. Finally, on 21 June the Siddons and Kemble left the Inchbalds for good when they set out for Liverpool, leaving the couple somewhat at loggerheads now they were abandoned suddenly to their own devices. However, they too soon left Birmingham on 29 June en route for Canterbury, where they were to stay in work for two months before finally achieving their ambition to join Tate Wilkinson's company.[18]

Tate Wilkinson was one of the most remarkable actor-managers in the English provincial theatre.[19] He was a great character and a law to himself. Born in 1739, he had trained with Garrick, but preferred being a big man in his own right in the north than competing for success in London. He set up a theatrical company with its chief centers of production in York and Hull, where he was responsible for establishing notable theatres with royal patents, and also playing regularly in Leeds and Wakefield. York had a population of some 24,000 in 1800 as against Bath, another great theatrical center in the provinces with its spa, which had a population by the end of the century of 30,000. In addition to being an actor-manager, Tate Wilkinson was a notable author and historian of the contemporary theatre, publishing his Memoirs in 1791 and The Wandering Patentee in 1795, the latter describing his experiences in Yorkshire from 1770 to 1795.

The Inchbalds were fortunate, therefore, to be hired by Tate Wilkinson. He believed in talent, and liked in addition to his regular, northern-based company, to introduce the London stars to his theatres to give his productions national status. He did much to rehabilitate Sarah Siddons' reputation as a great actress before her series of distinguished seasons in Bath, and

Elizabeth's seasons with him in the north from October 1777 preceded her final debut in London's Covent Garden in October 1780, two years before Sarah's outstanding triumph at Drury Lane in 1782.[20]

Under Tate Wilkinson's management the Inchbalds were to be reunited for a while with the Siddons, and in particular with Kemble in York.[21] Elizabeth and her husband began work, however, in Hull towards the end of October 1777, moving in January 1778 to York. Here West Digges was to make an appearance, and apparently paid sufficient attention to Elizabeth to create renewed jealousy in Joseph, while another far more humbly placed actor, Mr. Davis, who dressed Elizabeth's hair 'most zealously' on the nights she performed and 'seemed to live upon her smiles' and even lodged in the same house, roused further jealousy. In May they were moved by Wilkinson to Leeds, where Inchbald began scene-painting. Elizabeth received there a letter from Kemble, then another in Liverpool which refers to her literary activities:

> Now to your writings. Pray how far are you advanced in your novel? - what new characters have you in it - what situations? how many distressed damsels and valorous knights? how many prudes, how many coquettes? what libertines, what sentimental rogues in black and empty cut-throats in red? I must know all this whenever you write to this quarter again, which I hope will be soon. Write a little in French but at all events write often. You would, if you knew the pleasure I received from the good style, lively ideas, and polished manner of your letters.[22]

The main reference in Kemble's letter was to the initial version of Elizabeth's novel, A Simple Story, which she had begun drafting earlier in the year. One of Kemble's plays was a tragedy, Belisarius, which was turned down by Thomas Harris, the highly efficient manager of Covent Garden, but accepted by Tate Wilkinson for Hull. On 19 October Kemble arrived in Hull, and the play was presented with modest success on 29 December with Elizabeth in the cast. Their close friendship was renewed; however, in the words of Boaden, she later took care to record 'that he never was at any time her <u>lover</u>.'

It was in June 1779 that Elizabeth had to face the sudden and totally unexpected death of her husband at the age of only 44, while she herself was 25. The details of this are given by Boaden in his <u>Memoir</u> of Elizabeth:

> On the 4th of June they made an excursion to Halifax with a party (Mr. Inchbald on horseback), as usual with the fraternity, they had an eye to profit in their pleasures, and performed there that evening: the next day they returned home to Leeds, and on the following, suddenly, Mr. Inchbald expired, in consequence of some accident, probably an affection of the heart ...[23]

Boaden adds somewhat more in his <u>Memoirs</u> of Kemble:

> Mr. Inchbald had felt a slight indisposition, which his wife attributed to the day's heat, or a casual obstruction in the stomach. She had therefore recommended him to take some repose, and they had retired together, but he suddenly expired in her arms ...[24]

Although Elizabeth by now felt no remnants of romantic love for her husband, she was used to his company and valued what he had done to sustain her career, though they had always differed over her insistence on keeping under her own control as much of her earnings as possible, which enabled her to send presents, and perhaps money as well, to her mother in Standingfield. The day of her husband's sudden death she recollected as 'a day of horror,' and the week that followed one of 'grief, horror, and almost despair.' Kemble, a classical scholar, composed a lengthy inscription in Latin in which many of the dead man's virtues were extolled, including the assertions that he was an excellent father and faithful husband. George Inchbald joined Elizabeth in Leeds on 26 June and was engaged by Wilkinson; this helped her, but her constant companion was Kemble. Dr. Brodie was perhaps the first man actively to suggest that she consider marriage once again, writing to her from

19

London in July. It does not appear that Kemble did the same. It was, says Boaden, to become her practice to mold her lovers into lasting friends, and extinguish any hopes in them of marriage or sexual liaison. Boaden describes her attitude with modest elegance:

> The instances are not few of these repentant lovers being sobered into quiet, agreeable friends, frequently enjoying the charm of her society upon such conditions as she was pleased to impose. When a lady's charms lead their admirer to indiscretion, he has an advocate in her vanity, that at least breaks his fall. Actresses are more subjected to this species of annoyance than any other class of their sex; perhaps they are seen to have more attraction, and suspected of less rigor, than their sister charmers of the world.[25]

In October 1779, after discussing the first draft of her finished novel with Kemble and other friends, she sent it to Dr. Brodie to present to a publisher. He did so, but it was turned down. It was not in fact to be published, in what was to be a totally revised version, until 1791. It was a comfort therefore when Tate Wilkinson invited her to stay another year in the company at an increased salary of a guinea and a half a week. Her weekly expenses were normally under a pound. To this she could expect to add occasional 'benefit' performances which would bring in normally a further ten to fifteen pounds.[26] She was, in fact, comfortably off for a provincial actress; when her husband died, he left her with 252 pounds in investments and 128 pounds in cash. However, in her diary she recorded: 'Began this year a happy wife - finished it a wretched widow.'

Mrs INCHBALD.

From an Original Painting.

Published by J.Sewell, Cornhill.

Elizabeth Inchbald
Portrait published in 1807

II

DRAMATIST

Elizabeth Inchbald's first appearance on the London stage was to be at Covent Garden Theatre on 3 October 1780. The play was Fletcher's <u>Philaster</u>, and the part she played was Bellario, for which she wore male costume. This, says Boaden, suited her exactly; she 'looked the fond and faithful youth, with a loveliness that could not but interest.'[1] She had been interviewed by the Covent Garden manager, Thomas Harris, on Sunday 24 September, and engaged for a salary less than she had been getting from Tate Wilkinson, whose company she had left on 19 September, after appearing, since her husband's death in June 1779, for Wilkinson in Pontefract, York, Wakefield, Leeds, Hull and Doncaster. During much of the time her stepson, George Inchbald, remained a member of the company. She had had certain differences with Wilkinson, who knew that she was secretly approaching Harris in London with high hopes of being engaged at Covent Garden. During the summer of 1780 she had gone north to Edinburgh and, says Boaden, described herself as very unhappy at this time. She appeared on the stage in Edinburgh every night during race week, though for very little money. However, her lodgings there only cost her eight shillings a week.

Now that she was a young widow of 27, alone and unattached, she was made a fuss of and courted wherever she might be working or on holiday. Proposals for marriage (or liaison) began to develop as soon as the customary interval of six months' widowhood had elapsed after her husband's death. Kemble, it would seem, behaved circumspectly throughout; everyone, says Boaden, expected them to marry. But Kemble was essentially a very reserved, even a somewhat cold-natured young man, and as Boaden puts it:

> We think we know that Mr. Kemble
> could never have borne with the
> independent turn of her mind; he could
> never, we are sure, be blindly fond of

any woman; and, much as she might have respected him, she had a humour that demanded as much indulgence as that of her husband at least. Even as friends to the end of their lives, they had frequent differences, looking very like alienation.[2]

But other suitors were less reluctant. Dicky Suett, whose nickname was 'Gossip,' and who played clown parts, went so far as to approach Kemble to press an ill-judged suit with her. A certain Colonel Glover appears for a while to have been a favored visitor. In Edinburgh Elizabeth was surrounded by men who pressed their attentions upon her, including her former admirer, Mr. Sterling. She recorded that she was 'surprised' at the behavior of a Mr. Mason, and 'shocked a little' by the conversation of a Mr. Berkeley. A Sir John Whitefoord entered into a correspondence with her. Her Catholic friends began to be alarmed at what they considered to be her 'free course of life,' and one of her former women friends approached Dr. Alex Geddes to intervene with her, since it was evident she was neglecting her religious duties. Some part of Dr. Geddes' reply, dated 7 August, is of interest:

> I am very sensibly affected by what you tell me of Mrs. Inchbald, though I hope her situation is not quite so dangerous as to you it appears. From the little I know of her, I take her to be a woman of good sense, elegant manners, and gentle disposition; and it would give me great pain to think that her principles, as a Christian and a Catholic, did not entirely correspond with these amiable qualities ... I learn that she neither attends Mass on days of obligation, nor frequents the sacraments at times appointed.[3]

The Covent Garden company was a strong one, headed by John Henderson and Miss Younge, as well as on occasion Mrs. Mary Anne Yates, both of whom had been actresses with Garrick. Had Henderson not died young, at the age of 38, he would have become one of the great actors of the time. He had been established as a leading player in Bath, and had proved a good friend to Sarah Siddons, enabling her to join the company there, and acquit herself so well that her reputation took her back to Drury Lane in the autumn of 1782, where Kemble, her brother, joined her the year following.[4] Their joint acting careers were now to flourish in a brother and sister partnership the like of which remains unequalled in the history of the British theatre.

The years 1780-1786 saw the gradual change of Elizabeth's career from actress to dramatist. She remained with Harris's Covent Garden company for the 1780-81 and 1781-82 seasons, playing secondary roles at a very modest salary. In 1782 she undertook a summer season for George Colman the Elder's management at the Little Theatre, Haymarket, which had the license to present plays when the two Royal theatres remained closed. In 1782 she left Covent Garden to play her familiar leading parts again first in Shrewsbury during October and November, and afterwards in Dublin, where she remained until the end of May 1783, working there with Kemble. During the summer of 1783 she went back to the Haymarket for Colman, and created a minor sensation by appearing upon the stage without a wig and with her natural hair exposed. Boaden puts it handsomely:

> Our fair readers will like to be told, that Mrs. Inchbald, with equal economy, taste and purity, was among the first to try the effect of her natural hair upon the stage ... She absolutely appeared without powder; still, however, the natural shape of the human head was only to be guessed at, as at present, winged out by certain side-boxes of curls, and the head thus describing an equilateral triangle, of which the base was uppermost. Still to be rid of the larded meal was something ...[5]

Elizabeth was welcomed as an actress with modest praise in the London press; as Boaden puts it, she had to be 'content to twinkle in her humble sphere ... Mrs. Inchbald had but little freedom or grace in her action; she spoke, too, rather timidly than affectionately - rather emphatically than natural.' Her salary did not even twinkle; it rose

to two pounds a week , and then fluctuated between
two and three pounds according to the amount she
had to do. Colman reduced her to under two pounds
weekly, and during the summer she was forced to
rent a humble room for 3s6d a week. In Shrewsbury
(appearing twice a week) she received a guinea a
week, plus ten pounds for a benefit performance -
her board and lodging cost her in all eleven
shillings a week, with extra for tea and beer. In
Dublin she received five pounds a week, but three
pounds was deducted weekly against the takings of
her benefit performance, a very safe arrangement
for the management, especially as they deducted
thirty pounds from the performance, allowing her
only to keep the balance. In London she had been
very upset because Harris had insisted that she
walk on in pantomime, work beneath her status that
she hated. Nevertheless, she remained on
reasonable terms with Harris, and he kept her on as
a member of the Covent Garden company for the
seasons 1783-84 and 1784-85.

Elizabeth's somewhat straitened circumstances
made it harder than ever for her to maintain her
independence and refrain from accepting one of the
many offers of marriage she continued to receive
following the initial approaches of 'Dicky Gossip'
and the various other men who had come to see her
with mixed intentions. She received, for example,
letters of proposal from her old admirer, the actor
Richard Wilson. Dr. Brodie, too, renewed his suit,
though he became so importunate she had to refuse
him admittance to her residence. She went to a
masquerade with the Marquis of Carmarthen, but his
intentions (like that of most titled men with an
interest in actresses) were probably dubious.
Boaden quotes a marvelous story Elizabeth wrote
herself about the actresses at the Haymarket and
their admirers:

> To have fixed the degrees and
> shades of female virtue, possessed at
> this time by the actresses of the
> Haymarket Theatre, would have been
> employment for an able casuist. One
> evening, about half an hour before the
> curtain was drawn up, some accident
> having happened in the dressing-room of
> one of the actresses, a woman of known
> intrigue, she ran in haste to the

26

dressing-room of Mrs. Wells, to finish
the business of her toilet. Mrs. Wells,
who was the mistress of the well-known
Captain Topham, shocked at the intrusion
of a reprobated woman, who had a worse
character than herself, quitted her own
room, and ran to Miss Farren's crying,
'What would Captain Topham say, if I
were to remain in such company?' No
sooner had she entered the room, to
which as an asylum she had fled, than
Miss Farren flew out at the door,
repeating, 'What would Lord Derby say,
if I should be seen in such company?'[6]

A certain Mr. Glover, who was wealthy and
kept a carriage, offered Elizabeth five hundred
pounds a year if she would marry him. Sir Charles
Bunbury was another assiduous lover, but as Harris,
her manager, put it: 'That woman, Inchbald, has
solemnly devoted herself to <u>virtue</u> and a garret.'[7]
The witty Dr. John Walcot (Peter Pindar) celebrated
her virtue with this verse:

> Eliza, when with female art
> You seem to shun, and yet pursue,
> You act a false, a soul-less part,
> Unworthy love, unworthy you.
>
> Reluctance kills the rising bliss;
> Half-granted favours I disdain:
> The honey's lips that I would kiss,
> Are gall, unless they kiss again.
>
> No passive love, that silent takes
> All I can give without return:
> Be mine the frame that passion shakes;
> The liquid eye, the lips that burn.
>
> Desires that mantle in the face,
> Wishes that wait not to be won,
> The living dying, rapt embrace, -
> Give these delights, or give me none.[8]

In the end Elizabeth appears to have settled
for a platonic relationship with Sir Charles
Bunbury, and of course with Kemble - the only man
(it would seem) among her more assiduous admirers
who never came round to proposing - and, most
probably, the only one she might have accepted.[!]

27

Perhaps, suggests Boaden, he could not stand her
'rather haggard temper, which [she] could not but
show at intervals.'[9]

The form of independence to which she had
always looked forward was that of being a
successful writer. Unlike Sarah Siddons, she had
had (as we have seen) no formal schooling outside
her home, yet she could read earlier than her
brother George, who had been sent to school.
Elizabeth had made herself a highly literate woman,
though entirely self-educated. Her adolescent
ambition to be an actress had led her to study
plays (especially those of Shakespeare) which
contained the kind of parts she imagined she might
one day perform. Her reading in maturity included
in particular literature, biography and history,
and she annotated the books she read. In the
pocket-book diaries she maintained (so useful to
Boaden) she kept a record of these books, and they
reveal the ever-widening range of her interests.
Though traveling from town to town, rehearsing,
building up her repertoire of parts, committing
lines to memory when appearing in different plays
week by week, she still had some time in which to
read. She records while she was in Liverpool in
1777 she was reading Henry MacKenzie's sentimental
novel, The Man of Feeling (published anonymously in
1771), studying classical literature (including
Horace) translated into both French (in which she
became proficient after her visit to France the
previous year) and English, and absorbing Lord
Chesterfield's letters, Pope's Essay on Man, and Le
Sage's episodic novel, Gil Blas, which she read in
French.[10] The following year she was reading the
contemporary novel, Julia Mandeville 'as bearing on
her work,' Courtney Melmoth's Liberal Opinions, the
novel Jules de Roubigné, the letters of Dean Swift
and Goldsmith's The Vicar of Wakefield. Boaden
remarks that after her husband's death, 'she read a
great deal the latter half of 1779, chiefly to
divert her melancholy,' and she was, as we have
seen, already writing the first version of her own
novel, A Simple Story, at the time. By 1780 she
was still reading Pope - his Epistle of Eloisa to
Abelard sending her to the translated original
letters - and James Thomson's The Seasons. By 1782
she was studying English history, and also
astronomy. Boaden comments:

28

The *Catholic*, however, does not appear to have sensibly mixed in her present pursuits; and on the whole her mind was acquiring, not so much a Protestant, as a free or philosophical character. She studied a work on the globes, and entered carefully in her common-place book, the distances, bulk, and other characteristics of the heavenly bodies. She was accumulating too a good deal of natural philosophy, and by degrees had a readiness in the use of her stores that seemed rather the result of regular education, than the elements only gleaned by industrious maturity.[11]

She had a distinct taste for the classics, reading Pope's *Homer* and Dryden's *Vergil*. She read Swift's *Gulliver's Travels*, and in 1783 Rollin's *Ancient History of Greece* and *Rome*, Milton's *Paradise Lost* and *Paradise Regained*, Butler's *Hudibras*, Junius's *Letters*, Hume's *Essays*, the letters of Voltaire, Johnson's *Lives of the Poets* as well as Ovid and some of Plato's works in translation. Later she was to read Plutarch's *Lives*, and Aristotle. This was indeed a period when her lively and inquiring mind began to entertain doubts concerning the dogmas of her Church, and the sudden death of her husband and the decline and finally the death of her mother (to whom she was deeply attached) disturbed her faith. Her elder brother George and his wife, whose joint careers in the theatre had remained undistinguished, decided to take over management of the farm at Standingfield.

Elizabeth was left more than ever to discover new roots and friendships during the 1780s in London. She had commented on herself as early as 1776, when she was still only 22:

No other actual sin, but great coldness and imperfection in all my duties, especially in my religious ones, as in prayer and fasting.

And again:

Almighty God! look down upon thy
erring creature. Pity my darkness and
my imperfections, and direct me to the
truth! Make me humble under the
difficulties which adhere to my faith,
and patient under the perplexities which
accompany its practice.[12]

Although she and her husband were assiduous
churchgoers during their period together in
Canterbury, after his death we have already seen
how she neglected churchgoing in the social whirl
of her sojourn in Edinburgh during the summer of
1780. However, while staying with her mother in
Standingfield during the summer of 1781, Boaden
remarks that she 'now attended divine service
pretty regularly, which in London was omitted
altogether,' and when she was in Shrewsbury in 1782
en route to Dublin, she attended Mass every Sunday.

Her hopes turned increasingly on achieving
success through writing. A Simple Story - in its
original unpublished form begun in February 1777
but refused publication by the London publisher
Stockdale in spite of the intercession of her
admirer, Dr. Brodie - was put aside in favor of
more immediate work, plays which she could submit
for possible production to the London managers with
whom she worked, Thomas Harris at Covent Garden and
George Colman the Elder at the Little Theatre in
the Haymarket. In December 1779 Boaden says she
began work on a farce, and her mind was apparently
constantly sifting over plots for farces. In
December 1780 she had devised another on the
subject of polygamy, which she submitted to Harris
the following February; apparently he already had
two others and would make no decision. Eventually,
by March, she got the scripts back from him, the
plays unaccepted. She immediately sent one of
them, called The Ancient Law, to Colman, but he
also rejected it. In the same year she finished a
comedy and sent it to Colman - this too came to
nothing; he held on to it without offering any
response.

Still undaunted, Elizabeth conceived another
farce, which she called A Peep into a Planet -
according to Boaden, this was the original title of
the play which later brought her success, A Mogul

30

Tale, when it was eventually produced at the Haymarket in 1784. Harris, meanwhile, had raised her hopes by advancing her twenty pounds on a comedy. But there were other problems than acceptance of their work by the managers facing dramatists at the time - every play produced had to be granted a license by the Lord Chamberlain, and Sir Charles Bunbury proved helpful in getting this through at the end of August 1782. But we hear nothing more of this comedy, whereas A Mogul Tale was accepted by Colman, to whom she had submitted it in March 1784. According to Boaden, 'Colman complained of her writing saying, "he never met with so cramp a hand in his life."' He insisted on certain changes, however, which she carried out. On 23 June she took part in a first reading and was delighted the other members of the company liked her work. The play was presented on 6 July and, says Boaden, was a 'most brilliant success.' She notes herself: 'I played in The [sic] Mogul Tale, my own farce; it went off with the greatest applause.'[13] It was repeated ten times, and on 20 July she had her benefit performance, which realized some 77 pounds, and Colman added some 27 pounds; the whole totalled a hundred guineas for her. Kemble, still working for Tate Wilkinson in the north, sent her an elegant letter of congratulation from Leeds on 17 July:

> I cannot pay you a compliment in verse too high for what I truly think of you in prose; and I might tell you, that poetry is too essentially fictitious to answer the purpose of real esteem, and to express deserved praise....Your regular and continent life gives you the assurance of many healthful years; and your uncommon talents, having now forced themselves into notice, will crown you with growing reputation. If I could write, I would; I cannot - so you must receive esteem instead of flattery, and sincerity for wit, when I swear there is no _woman_ I more truly admire, nor any _man_ whose abilities I more highly esteem.[14]

Elizabeth had withheld her name as author of the farce, and she appeared in it in the part of Selina. She was so nervous on the opening night she

was at one moment transfixed on the stage. Boaden
tells the story:

> While she was standing in her
> natural alarm upon the stage, as Selina,
> in the second scene, she heard a cue
> from another character, Atkins the
> shoemaker, after which she was herself
> to speak. The cue was, 'Since we left
> Hyde Park Corner.' She had merely to
> reiterate as an exclamation, 'Hyde Park
> Corner!' but terror had robbed her
> entirely of utterance; she turned pale,
> and remained for a time in a suspension
> of mute amazement. At length, with a
> stammer which in private only attended
> her, she slowly, and in a sepulchral
> voice, ejaculated, 'Hh-yde Pa-ark
> Co-orner!' to the great astonishment and
> derision of many; and probably, though
> an emotion disproportioned to the
> occasion, there might be some who
> considered it as the most natural
> exclamation they ever heard from the
> stage in their lives. However, her own
> humour soon pealing in upon the
> audience, they were hurried on into the
> heartiest bursts of laughter that they
> had enjoyed for a long time.[15]

The money she received enabled her to pay a
long-standing debt to her faithful hair-dresser,
Davis, the man who had been one of the causes of
jealousy during her husband's lifetime. Davis was
employed by other actresses than Elizabeth, as
Boaden describes, addressing his women readers:

> Mr. Davis, ladies, had the honour
> of being first minister of state to
> several empresses of the
> Theatres-Royal. He was accordingly
> closeted, three and four hours together,
> with that astonishing artist Mrs.
> Abington, whose taste presided over
> courts and birthdays, and all polite
> assemblies. He was not equally wanted
> by Miss Younge, but extremely welcome to
> her toilet; and to Mrs. Inchbald's he
> had a similar access; to which, for
> years, we may add her tea, and dinner,

and supper table, where they sat like
<u>nature</u> and <u>art</u>, combined in some novel
manner together. Davis was treated by
the ladies as if they never thought of
his <u>sex</u>; and a more simple and
well-intentioned creature never
ministered at the shrine of vanity. He
contrived their dresses, and he dressed
the wearers of them, until the last
glance pronounced the labour of
enchantment accomplished.

Elizabeth owed him some 44 pounds in fees over the
years, and she paid him.

The success of <u>A Mogul Tale</u> emboldened
Elizabeth to remind Colman he had had for some
while a comedy of hers in his possession,
apparently unread. (Whether this is the comedy
originally submitted to Harris is not clear.)
Colman now read the script, suggested 'a world of
changes,' but agreed to present it - indeed, he
later gave it his own title of <u>I'll Tell You What</u> -
a title she did not like but did not attempt to
have changed. Elizabeth took up his suggestions
for changes during the winter, returning the
revisions in March after receiving advice from
another friend, Francis Twiss, later to become
Kemble's brother-in-law, who read with her during
the evenings while she went to dine with him on
Sundays. Kemble too, once he was back in London at
Drury Lane in the autumn of 1783, became once more
a constant visitor. <u>I'll Tell You What</u> was finally
presented by Colman in July 1785, but this time
Elizabeth was not in the cast. The play was very
favorably received, so much so that Elizabeth's
exacting friend Twiss felt it necessary to warn her
against the adverse effects of too much
ill-considered praise. Writing from Norwich, he
said:

Now the report of ... George Colman
is favourable, but I am sure he never
uttered any of the nonsense which other
people insulted you with (for such
extravagant eulogiums deserve no other
name), as he too well knows the
difference between <u>The School for
Scandal</u> and <u>I'll Tell You What</u>.
However, let him express himself in what

33

terms of commendation he will, (for that other high-flown stuff you must yourself know to be too ridiculous), my opinion will not be changed on that account. Should it become the most popular piece on the stage, I should not be mortified, but rejoice on your account....Your piece does not sufficiently live in my memory to enable me to enter into a regular criticism. As to the language of the serious part, I again repeat, that what you call simple and unaffected, I consider as low and grovelling; and that the pathos of the scene (at least my feelings spoke so) is not a little impaired by the humility of the style. As for the rest, I think it a pretty, light, summer piece, likely to pay you very well for the time and anxiety you have undergone.[16]

The play earned Elizabeth three hundred pounds, though Colman didn't buy the copyright. The following October Twiss and Kemble walked with her to the city to purchase stock - four hundred pounds in the 3 per cents, for which she paid some two hundred and forty pounds. She was always to be careful with money - it represented her independence, though when she had the means she was generous to her numerous family connections.

Her next play, Appearance is Against Them, though refused by Colman, was nevertheless adopted by Harris, and played at Covent Garden in October 1785. The King asked for it, and the Prince of Wales went to see it. It was indeed the first of her plays to appear in print - her publisher being George Robinson, who was henceforth to publish her plays regularly. He bought the copyright as well for her next farce, The Widow's Vow (an adaptation of a successful play in France, L'heureuse Erreur, by M. Patrat), which was presented by Colman at the Little Theatre, Haymarket on 20 June 1786. The Widow's Vow turned, in Boaden's words, on 'an ambiguity of sex,' and Colman, when accepting it, wrote in March from Bath:

I have just run over your farce, and think I never received or read any piece on which I could so immediately and

34

decidedly pronounce that it would do;
and do, as I think, with little or no
alteration.[19]

In 1787 her next play, Such Things Are, was
taken by Harris for Covent Garden and performed in
February. Robinson bought the copyright for
publication, and it received royal patronage on 19
February. The King and the Queen and the three
princesses were 'greatly delighted,' and Elizabeth
was to claim it brought her some nine hundred
pounds. She was now beginning to be recognized as
an established playwright who could count on being
able to exist by her pen, and by the 1790s she was
to employ a good broker called Morgan to handle her
stock and purchase the annuities on which she
managed to eke out a modest existence without, at
least by the end of the 1780s, being any longer
forced to work as an actress.

From 1787 to 1811 Elizabeth was in continuous
literary and editorial production. In all she
completed 21 plays, 11 of which were original
compositions, the rest free adaptations from
various French dramatists[20] and in two instances
from the German of the dramatist Kotzebue.[21] In
October 1787 she had her thirty-fourth birthday,
and her literary career was to last until she was
approaching 60. She finally retired from acting in
1789, and then devoted herself to the continuous
professional writing of plays and novels, and from
1805 to 1811 to the editing of the three series of
British plays published in association with her
name: The British Theatre (25 volumes of five
plays each, 1806-9, originally published as part
works with biographical and critical
introductions), her collection in ten volumes, The
Modern Theatre (1809), comprising 50 plays, and her
Collection of Farces and Afterpieces (also 1809)
made up of seven volumes, involving 63 plays in
all. Boaden claims that when she retired from
acting her income from her savings was 58 pounds a
year. Her independence was life itself to her, but
although relatively well established as a dramatist
by the end of the decade, she could only afford to
live very modestly in the rooms she rented in
London. Her home in Frith Street, writes Boaden,
'was a single room up two pair of stairs, in which
she sat with her shutters closed, that her
attention might be rigidly confined to her

35

business.' She refused an acting engagement at Drury Lane offered her by Sheridan and Kemble. Boaden tells us that she lived parsimoniously on twenty-five shillings a week.

Her private life was one of intense literary activity punctuated by a continual social round, a pattern she was to follow for the next ten years or more provided she was in good health. She was always to live humbly in rented rooms which she changed frequently according to her needs and fortunes; she entertained regularly, and as frequently visited her friends, the most assidious in 1787-88 including Sir Charles Bunbury, the Kembles, Harris, and M. Le Texier, Harris's agent for procuring likely plays from France which Elizabeth adapted in English, usually against the clock to meet Harris's persistent demands.[22] Her health, it must always be remembered, tended to be indifferent (as was the case with many gentlefolk, especially women, in the 18th century); nevertheless, she had the stamina to work hard: she produced, for instance, the play <u>Child of Nature</u> on Harris's urgent demand in ten days, as Boaden records:

> No time was to be lost; she immediately locked herself up, closed her shutters, and was denied to every human being till she had completed her translation in four acts. In ten days this indefatigable spirit accomplished it, and on the 11th of September wrote to Mr. Harris stating her terms.[23]

Following a bout of 'face-ache,' and an abcess on her leg at the end of the year 1789, she began to visit and be visited by a Dr. Warren who attended her as a physician, and as a result started what Boaden calls 'one of her most <u>interesting</u> friendships.' Perhaps she was affected by the marriage of Kemble to the actress, Priscilla Hopkins in December 1787. Even in her thirties, the virtuous, independent Elizabeth could suffer from susceptibility, and it would seem, as we shall see, she was soon to form some kind of infatuation for Dr. Warren, who was a married man. At their initial meeting she recorded that 'he behaved sweetly.' As Boaden puts it, he 'absolutely won her heart by his kindness: he called as a friend...

The merit of her character seems to have been irresistible.' On the other hand, her near relatives began to become something of a trouble to her, and in this area 1788-89 were to be difficult years:

> Her sister Dolly had been residing in Standingfield, but their brother George had gone wrong in his affairs, and there was an end to that accommodation for her; she came accordingly to London, to live as she could for a time, chiefly we may be sure upon her sister Inchbald. Debby, who was prettier than Mrs. Inchbald, and lived, perhaps, as bar-maid, with a Mr. Luttrel, called upon her occasionally; sometimes she got money from her, at others was refused admission. The two sons of her excellent husband besieged her by letter; but she refused to see either of them this year.[24]

Both Dolly and Debbie had an increasingly hard time to survive, and Elizabeth was forced constantly to help them. Debbie died in 1794, and Elizabeth's brother George perished the following year, shot dead in a duel.[25]

Occupied in 1789 as she was with translations for Le Texier and Colman, as well as starting to write original work, she managed to resume work on A Simple Story, adding substantial material to it, as we shall see. It was accepted in its final form by her regular publisher, Robinson, who paid two hundred pounds for the rights, was published in 1791, running immediately into a second edition.

Her infatuation for Dr. Warren bears some resemblance to her adolescent 'crush' on the actor Richard Griffith. She did not attempt to hide her feelings from Boaden:

> If she hears his name in company, she is delighted with the word; and she records her practice of continually walking up and down Sackville Street, where he lived, watching whether there were lights in his apartments – following his carriage about town, for

the chance of seeing him - and other
extravagances....The very stones of
Sackville Street might cry out upon the
repeated efforts of his fair patient to
catch a glimpse of him. One morning she
was told, before breakfast, that a print
of the doctor was to be seen in a
shop-window; she immediately went to
look at it; a few days afterwards she
bought it, and was charmed with it; the
next day writes - 'Read, worked, and
looked at my print;' and yet we should
suspect it was herself that she really
loved.[26]

An oddly psychological remark, that, for Boaden to
make.

One of her biggest successes of the 1790s
resulted from her comedy, Every One Has His Fault,
which was presented at Covent Garden in January
1793. Published by Robinson, it had a wide sale.
It is in connection with this play that some public
discussion of Elizabeth's political liberalism
begins to be aired. The play was attacked in a
highly conservative journal, The True Briton.
Boaden, commenting on the success of the play when
published in February 1793, writes:

The sale was immense, for the 'True
Briton' had been idle enough to make a
political attack upon the doctrines it
espoused, as tending to
disorganization. This journal was
established for the avowed object of
supporting Mr. Pitt in his endeavours to
suppress the revolutionary spirit, then
systematically exerting itself against
the governments of all countries. They
heard therefore with alarm anything like
liberal opinions delivered with an
emphasis upon the public stage, and
caught up enthusiastically by the
people, as sanctioning inferences that
went still farther.[27]

Elizabeth felt the need to publish a reply on 1
February 1793 in a journal called The Diary:

After the most laborious efforts

38

to produce a dramatic work deserving the approbation of the town; after experiencing the most painful anxiety till that approbation was secured; a malicious falsehood, aimed to destroy every advantage arising from my industry, has been circulated in a print called 'The True Briton,' in which I am accused of conveying seditious sentiments to the public. This charge I considered of little importance, while an impartial audience were, every evening, to judge of its truth:- but my accuser having, in this day's paper, taken a different mode of persecution, saying I have expunged those sentences which were of dangerous tendency, the play can, now, no longer be its own evidence: I am, therefore, compelled to declare, in contradiction to this assertion, that not one line, or one <u>word</u>, has been altered or omitted since the first night of representation.[28]

Not all her later plays of the 1790s carried such implications. Among her successes of the period were the delightful farce, <u>The Wedding Day</u> (1794), <u>Wives as They Were and Maids as They Are</u> (1797), and her adaptations of Kotzebue's plays, <u>Lovers' Vows</u> (Kotzebue's 'Child of Love,' 1798) and <u>The Wise Man of the East</u> (Kotzebue's 'The Writing Desk,' 1799).[29]

In connection with this last play interesting letters survive that show not only Elizabeth's methods of work but her acute business sense. Harris had given her a rough translation of Kotzebue's text which she set about adapting radically for the English stage. She wrote to Harris on 29 August:

Sir, According to your desire I send you the terms, as fairly as my calculation can make them, on which it will be worth my while to hazard the success of the German play I have been altering; and if there should be any thing in my demand which does not meet with your perfect concurrence, I will most willingly submit to the arbitration

39

of any two persons you and I shall appoint, and suffer that our agreement be regulated by their judgment.

I ask one hundred pounds on the third, one hundred on the sixth, and one hundred on the ninth night of the representation of the play; making in the whole three hundred pounds. For every night it is played after, during twenty-one nights, which will exactly include the thirtieth, I ask twenty pounds a night.

This will make my demand on the theatre three hundred pounds for the first nine nights, five hundred and twenty on the twentieth night's performance, and seven hundred and twenty pounds should the play be so fortunate as to run thirty nights.

For the above proposals I reserve to myself the sale of my own altered manuscript; but which manuscript, whatever good success may attend the play, you may purchase of me, at any time previous to the third night, to two hundred pounds; which is the sum I received for 'Lovers Vows,' at the late date of the twenty-third night, when it was first published, and had many original manuscripts published six weeks prior to it to injure its value.

I beg leave to mention that this play has given me equal trouble of invention that any one wholly my own ever did; and that I have gained more by one of my own on the twentieth night, than I could now gain upon the thirtieth; and that the original manuscript will be saleable in proportion to the success of mine, and no doubt will repay the demands of the original author.[30]

Harris in the end settled for a payment of five hundred pounds, which Elizabeth wisely accepted. On the day she delivered the script to Harris she wrote to her friend, Mrs. Phillips:

The complaint of weakness and excessive pain in my legs is returned, and I now consider it as the effect of sitting fifteen hours a day, for ten weeks past, at the German play of Kotzebue's, in which I have exerted all my strength, both of body and mind. At the end, Mr. Harris has not treated me as I expected. My verbal agreement was, that I should have the same reward as if the piece had been wholly my own; but having once sold a play of my own, before it was acted, to him for five hundred pounds, he wished to make that sum the estimate of my present payment. After some contention, I this day gave up my altered manuscript for that price; though had I run the risk I wished to run, the sum in case of success had been double....where money is the subject, I feel great delicacy, and had rather receive too little than too much: but not anything can pay me for the loss of health.[31]

Elizabeth's association with the actor and author Thomas Holcroft and with William Godwin - both of whom, it would seem, at one stage or another wanted to marry her - will be the subject of further discussion, since the influence of their radical, liberalizing opinions came to a head in her two novels, A Simple Story (1791) and Nature and Art (written in 1794 and published 1796) as well as in certain of her plays, including very obviously The Massacre (1792), a short tragedy in three acts 'taken from the French' but never acted and even after having been printed, withdrawn from publication 'in deference to political opinions,' as Boaden puts it. It was not to be published until 1833, when Boaden included it in the first volume of his Memoirs of Mrs. Inchbald.

Although she recorded that she attended Mass regularly in 1792, and that (in Boaden's words) 'she prayed and made an examination of her conscience,' she possibly did so because she was in process of rethinking her position, initially under the influence of Thomas Holcroft. Holcroft was at the very center of what came to be termed the Jacobin movement in the literature and thinking of the 1790s. Born in 1745, he was eight years older than Elizabeth, and was later to be best known for

41

his melodrama, <u>The Road to Ruin</u>, (1791). Son of an impoverished pedlar, he had been in turn stableboy, cobbler, teacher and finally actor, dramatist and author. In 1784 he had visited Paris, and his familiarity with Beaumarchais's <u>Marriage of Figaro</u> led to success for his translation of the play, <u>The Follies of a Day</u> (1784) in which, as an actor, he had played Figaro. He was a convinced radical and supporter of the French Revolution, and in 1794 he was tried and convicted of high treason, but imprisoned for only two months. Among those who visited him in prison were his friends, Godwin and Elizabeth.

Holcroft was therefore closely associated with what came to be called the Jacobin movement in the literature of the 1790s. He was the first to exercise some influence on Elizabeth, and she submitted the revised text of <u>A Simple Story</u> to him to criticize and, according to Boaden, Elizabeth was in August 1789 'correcting her novel by his suggestions.' Holcroft, a volatile man, sent her 'a very passionate and supplicating letter' (her own description) to which (it would seem) she replied coolly. Holcroft, however, only gave up for the time being. Much later, in August 1793, after the novel's publication and the suppression of <u>The Massacre</u>, Elizabeth records that he called and stayed for some time, presenting her with 'verses upon his passion' and, she says, 'wrongfully reproached her for her behaviour.' He was then in his later forties, and she almost into hers. Did he know that she was experiencing a similar ardor in her infatuation for Dr. Warren? Warren was constantly in her thoughts and Boaden says, quoting her own words, 'when she is so happy as to meet him ' "she is afraid to look at him" – sometimes absolutely <u>avoids</u> him, though she has been waiting for his arrival.' Another admirer, the oculist John Taylor, 'had the tenderest regard for her,' says Boaden, adding that, 'Taylor with great sincerity told her to beware of her politics, as their apparent leaning might injure her fortune.' Taylor was not alone in such warnings. Boaden writes: 'she used to receive anonymous letters occasionally, of <u>caution</u>...and many personal friends, besides Taylor, ventured to admonish the independent lady.'

Elizabeth's friendship with William Godwin

had begun in 1792. She submitted the script of A Simple Story to him, and also her play, The Massacre. Godwin, born in 1756, was three years younger than Elizabeth; author, intellectual and rationalist philosopher, he had had a Calvinistic upbringing, and was for a while a minister until he came under the influence of French philosophical rationalism, joining with Thomas Holcroft and others in promoting the idea of drastic social reform and revolution. His most celebrated work was to be The Enquiry Concerning the Principles of Political Justice (1793), and his novels Caleb Williams (1794) and St. Leon (1799) reflected his changing views during the 1790s. He opposed all forms of government (and especially the monarchical) which he held to threaten and ultimately destroy the perfectibility of man, together with the poison of religion and misconceived forms of education as experienced in contemporary European society, all of which he held to lead only to corruption. He advocated the rule of reason, which power politics aims to stifle, as well as the abolition of all censorship or repression of opinion, and he favored an enlightened, benevolent treatment of the criminal. He also opposed the marriage contract; man and woman, uncorrupted, should live together freely in terms of mutual respect. In 1797 he was to marry Mary Wollstonecraft, whom he had first met only the year before and who had come to live with him and was pregnant by him. They went through the ceremony of marriage against their principles in order to legitimize their child. Ten days after giving birth to Mary Godwin (the poet Shelley's future wife, and the author of Frankenstein) she died. Elizabeth's attitude to Mary Wollstonecraft was to lead to a rift with Godwin.[32]

Elizabeth submitted the script of A Simple Story to Godwin as well as to Holcroft for criticism, as we have seen. She also sent him The Massacre, her only tragedy which, though set in 17th century France, had obvious contemporary references to the grave events which were taking place in that country at this very time, and deeply affecting alike those in favor of reform and those opposed to it in nearby Britain. The revolutionary divisions came to a head in France during the period 1789 (the year of the fall of the Bastille) and 1793 (the year of the execution of the French

King, Louis XVI, and his Queen, the much-hated
Austrian, Marie-Antoinette). Louis, a vacillating
and basically weak man, had remained obstinately
head of state when the whole constitution was
crumbling and the foundations of a republic were
being established, phase by phase. These events
had naturally enough profound repercussions in
Britain, both on those who supported the status quo
and those who favored varying degrees of liberal
reform and, whether extremist or not, were termed
Jacobins for their pains. Opinions were obviously
deeply divided about what was happening in France,
and the summary execution of the King and Queen
acted like a shock-wave throughout the realm,
sharpening alike conservative and radical opinion.
1791 had seen the ignominious flight of the royal
family in disguise from Paris, their arrest at
Varennes and their virtual house imprisonment in
the Tuileries in June. The Jacobins, representing
the extremists in the advancement of social reform
and the establishment of their concept of civil
rights, became the primary force that led to the
invasion of the Tuileries in 1792, the suspension
of the monarchy, and the imprisonment of the royal
family. Their execution was followed by the
September massacres of royalists, aristocrats, and
priests. By 1793 the Jacobins had taken charge of
France, and the conservatives in Britain were
determined to stamp out all tendencies to
liberalism and radicalism alike as the equivalent
of high treason.

For a while at least Elizabeth was partially
caught up in the radical fervor which was
represented in Britain by such writers as Godwin
and Holcroft. One of Elizabeth's more devoted (and
firmly married) 'literary friends' (Boaden's
phrase), George Hardinge - some of whose
elaborately gallant but undated letters of the
period addressed to his 'dear Muse' Boaden
reproduces - reproves her for her dangerous
sentiments expressed in a letter she had sent him.
He wrote to her:

> Your most absurd letter, just
> received, shall never appear in judgment
> against you: not because it is
> ill-natured and unjust, - not because it
> convinces me that your temper is
> impracticable (because these are points

that are becoming and rather interesting
in a <u>petticoat</u>), but from the delicacy
that <u>I</u> feel for <u>you</u>, and which <u>you</u>
little deserve: in other words, because
it is a childish and weak letter. It
has the head of bigotry, and the soul of
Holcroft....As for your <u>abuse</u>, you have
taught me to value it. Oh that I may
for ever be called <u>stupid</u> by the person
who wrote a <u>Satire upon the Times</u>, by
setting a ship on fire, and burning
every soul in the book except a Lord of
the Bed-chamber - by whom she meant the
King.[33]

Elizabeth's <u>Satire upon the Times</u> does not survive,
and Boaden writes dismissively of it - 'it must
allude to some of those political writings which
were of a temporary nature, and have happily
perished in the furious season that gave birth to
them.' Boaden was in fact out in the <u>Memoirs</u> to
hush up as much as he could those dangerous
tendencies in Elizabeth's writings as unsuiting to
her, and her relationships with both Holcroft and
Godwin are given scant attention considering how
important they were.

Evaluation of the Plays

        Elizabeth in all wrote 21 plays - one tragedy
(<u>The Massacre</u>), 12 farces and light comedies, and
eight serious comedies. Three of these were never
published - <u>All on a Summer's Day</u> (1787) and <u>The</u>
<u>Hue and Cry</u> (1791) exist only in manuscript in the
Larpent Collection at the Huntington Library in
California. The third, <u>Young Men and Old Women</u>
(1792), for long thought lost, is claimed by
Allardyce Nicoll to survive in an anonymous script
in the Larpent Collection titled <u>Lovers No</u>
<u>Conjurers</u>. (See Appendix Two). All the others
(bar two) were published singly between 1785 and
1805; the two exceptions were <u>A Case of Conscience</u>
(1800; never acted), which Boaden published in the
second volume of the <u>Memoirs of Mrs. Inchbald</u>, and
<u>The Massacre</u> (1792), which should have been
published and was indeed set by the printers but
withdrawn from publication by Elizabeth. A rare
copy is held by the Library of Congress. Boaden
rescued the text and published it in volume one of

the <u>Memoirs</u>.

Of the 21 plays, eight (<u>The Widow's Vow</u>,
1786; <u>The Midnight Hour</u>, 1787; <u>Animal Magnetism</u> and
<u>The Child of Nature</u>, 1788; <u>The Married Man</u>, 1789;
<u>The Hue and Cry</u> and <u>Next Door Neighbours</u>, 1791;
<u>Young Men and Old Women</u>, 1792) owed their origin to
popular French originals, though mostly very freely
adapted, and two more (<u>Lovers' Vows</u>, 1798; <u>The Wise
Man of the East</u>, 1799) were taken, very loosely,
from Kotzebue. For example, the libertine Count
Cassel in <u>Lovers' Vows</u> is an invention of
Elizabeth. The rest of Elizabeth's plays were
original. Whether composing original plays or
making adaptations, she used great variety of
location; though the majority are set in or near
London, five have Spanish settings, and two are set
in the Orient. <u>The Massacre</u> is naturally set in
France, while <u>Lovers' Vows</u>, coming from Kotzebue,
is set in Germany. Characters, too, are very
frequently introduced who return to England after a
long spell abroad - such as Sir William Dorrillon
in <u>Wives as They Were</u>, Lavensforth (accompanied by
his faithful black servant, Amos) in <u>To Marry or
not to Marry</u>, Baron Wildenheim in <u>Lovers' Vows</u>, and
Count Orviedo and his servant Girone in <u>A Case of
Conscience</u>, Irwin and his wife, Lady Eleanor in
<u>Everyone has his Fault</u>, Euston and his brother
Anthony in <u>I'll Tell You What</u>, and Tom Contest in
<u>The Wedding Day</u> - to say nothing of the intrepid
balloonists in <u>A Mogul Tale</u>, who have little chance
to escape from the Mogul's clutches and return home
until the very end of the play. The use of foreign
names and settings was as romantically infectious
in the 18th century as it had been in Elizabethan
times two centuries earlier, and there was
particular emphasis now on the Far East in
Elizabeth's plays, as indeed there was in her
novel, <u>Nature and Art</u>.

Seeing that the plays are so lively and
contemporary in dialogue - suggesting 'real life'
as immediately as Jane Austen was to do in her
novels - it is strange that Elizabeth felt unable
to abandon the use of type-names, a device that
begins to date badly by the end of the 18th
century. Not only does it suggest that the old
'humours' psychology still tended to flourish in
this form, but it also must have led to the
maintenance of type-casting and type-performance.

It would be difficult to bring 'psychological realism' or 'acting in depth' to bear when playing characters so obviously oriented round types as Mr. Bluntly, the honest adviser, or the wealthy spendthrift, Sir George Splendorville, or the unscrupulous lawyer, Mr. Blackman, all in Next Door Neighbours, or the astute businessman, Tradewell Classick (the Classick part of the name referring to his brother's love of books) and the womanizing Lord Lovemore, or the libertine Lord Rakeland in The Wedding Day, or Messrs. Placid and Harmony in Everyone has his Fault or Mr. Bankwell in Wise Man of the East. Such Things Are bristles with these character-names - Sir Luke and Lady Tremor, or Lord Flint, hard-hearted agent of the Sultan. With or without such obvious indications of temperamental bias, set piece characterizations abound throughout the plays: harsh fathers, craftily intriguing servants, libertine lords; though some of the libertines reform at the end of the play, such as Sir George Splendorville, others, like Count Valentia in The Child of Nature and Count Cassel in Lovers' Vows, do not.

In the lighter plays and farces, which have little or no pretension to some special comic significance, plots are continually contrived out of intrigue, concealed identity and prolonged misunderstandings. They have roots in Terence and Plautus. Angry fathers or guardians are deceived or tricked by their romantically-inclined offspring or wards, who are invariably seeking union with forbidden lovers. Servants are only too willing to become involved in the deception, having (usually) loves themselves among servants in one or other of the various households involved. Thus intrigue piles upon intrigue until the climax brings some happy resolution at the end. What makes Elizabeth's light entertainments superior to most of the kind surviving from the period is the high quality of her dialogue and her adroit handling of situations. Her happy endings can be as far-fetched and contrived as Shakespeare's, but audiences in the 18th century remained willing to accept such dramatic conventions. After all, opera-goers accept them to this day. Theatre-goers were interested in the immediate performances of beloved star-players scene by scene, and were scarcely overcritical about the outcome of the action.[34] However, Genest in his published records

of annual production in the British theatre does
not hesitate to criticize what he regards as
over-contrivance, and Twiss, in his detailed
strictures on plot and dialogue written to
Elizabeth in private was equally concerned with
verisimilitude and tidiness of plot.[35]

About half of Elizabeth's plays depend on
intrigue, concealed identity and aggravated
misunderstanding. For example, among the lighter
entertainments and farces: The Widow's Vow (1786)
turns on the deception practiced on a beautiful
widow who (after an unhappy marriage) is determined
to refuse the company and even the sight of men;
nevertheless she accepts marriage once more quite
graciously when she has been actually tricked into
receiving a would-be lover disguised as a woman,
while The Married Man (1789) involves the
inevitable embarrassments and confusions that
follow on a married recluse refusing to acknowledge
that he is actually married to the beautiful woman
who lives in his household and who is, in
consequence of her apparent unattached state,
pursued by would-be lovers under his nose. In The
Wedding Day (1794), one of Elizabeth's liveliest
farces, misunderstandings follow when the elderly
Lord Adam Contest makes no secret of resenting the
behavior of his youthful bride with other men,
after he has offended her on their wedding day by
making it abundantly clear she does not measure up
to his memories of his former wife.

Even the 'serious' comedies are not above
similar contrivances of plot. Once again,
Shakespeare offered a model in his more serious,
later comedies, such as Measure for Measure and
All's Well that Ends Well, in both of which an
extreme form of sexual deception is involved, a
woman in earnest pursuit of a man entering his bed
in the guise of the particular woman after whom he
lusts. In Such Things Are (1787) a woman prisoner
confined over the years in the Sultan's noisome
prison turns out to be the long-lost love for whom
he has been vainly seeking. In Lovers' Vows (1798)
it emerges that the young veteran home from the
wars is the illegitimate son of the local Baron,
and that the penniless mother he strives in vain to
support is no less than the woman the Baron (now a
widower) once seduced and still may love. The Wise
Man of the East (1799) turns on the identity of the

mysterious 'wise man,' Ava Theanoa, now on a visit to England; he appears to come from Cambodia, but at the end of the play turns out to be Clarensforth's father in disguise. The complex plot of A Case of Conscience (1800-01) concerns the loss of affection by a Spanish marquis for his wife and son, and also the identity of a hermit, Salvador, living in relative seclusion nearby. Salvador is in fact the Duke Cordunna, the man to whom the Marquise had been betrothed before deserting him to marry the Marquis. To Marry or Not to Marry (1805) involves the concealed identity of a young girl Mrs. Mortland takes under her protection and who manages to attract the attention of her brother, who likes to be thought a confirmed bachelor.

The serious comedies, as distinct from the lighter entertainments, are distinguished by their frequent satiric handling of social and other issues. Elizabeth constantly returns to the social themes that concern her - the sharp contrasts arising from extremes of wealth and poverty, and the consequent injustices and undeserved sufferings that result, the problems of marriage both as a social institution and as a loving, or not so loving, relationship, the desire for independence shown by men and women alike, and the consequent plain speaking in matters of moral and social values that independence involves.

Several of the plays emphasize the evils of poverty and deprivation. In Next Door Neighbours (1791), while Sir George Splendorville, Lady Caroline Splendorville and their friends squander money in gambling as a matter of course, Harry and his sister Eleanor live next door in acute poverty in a rented room owned by the unscrupulous lawyer, Blackman. Their father, too, languishes in a debtors' prison, and Eleanor is soon to receive unwelcome attentions from Sir George, the natural prey of the rich man as a result of her destitution. Everyone has his Fault (1793) involves the problems of the impoverished Irwin and his wife, Eleanor; Irwin is eventually driven to steal Lord Norland's pocketbook in the street, little realizing Norland is his father-in-law. In Wise Man of the East (1799) the Metlands' poverty is shown up in marked contrast to the squanderings of Clarensforth, spendthrift son of the man to whom

Metland had once entrusted his only capital the very day the elder Clarensforth was to die, his property (and it is believed Metland's cash) destroyed by fire. Maria and her companion in Wives as they Were (1797) run up gambling and other debts only to find themselves eventually confined in a debtors' prison. It would seem in all these as well as in certain other plays, like Lovers' Vows (1798) - in which the discarded mistress of the wealthy Baron Wildenheim and the soldier son she had by him are forced to beg in the streets - that Elizabeth is concerned to stress the basic injustice which such uneven distribution of wealth entails, forcing only too often the deprived to resort to violence in order to provide the basic necessities of their dependents.

Since Elizabeth herself had scarcely enjoyed an ideal marriage, the problems of husbands and wives occupy many of the plays. They are most obvious in the case of the Placids, who are always at loggerheads in Everyone has his Fault (1793), in the bickerings of the elderly Sir Adam and his overyouthful wife from the very day of their marriage (The Wedding Day, 1794), in the satiric study of the autocratic Lord Priory and his absurdly overcompliant lady in Wives as They Were (1797), and in the suffering imposed on Adriana by the false suspicions of a jealous and vengeful husband in A Case of Conscience (1800-01). There are people in Everyone has his Fault who blow hot and cold over getting married, like Mr. Solus and Miss Spinster, and Sir Robert Ramble, who has divorced his wife after seven years of marriage during which he has neglected her for six. Divorce, too, creates the comic situation in one of the earliest and sharpest of Elizabeth's light comedies, I'll Tell You What (1785), in which Major Cyprus, having successfully seduced Sir George Euston's wife, Lady Harriet, and subsequently got married to her, finds the tables turned on him when Euston becomes his former wife's lover and so is in the happy position of being able to cuckold Cyprus.

In The Widow's Vow (1786), the Countess refuses even to receive a man in her presence after the disappointment she has experienced following her first marriage, which she and everyone else had regarded as a love match. In The Married Man (1789), Sir John Classick is doing everything he can to conceal his secret marriage to a pretty, if penniless girl, claiming that marriage only robs a man of his dignity, while Sir Oswin Mortland in To Marry or not to Marry (1805) is that most comic of comic characters, the confirmed bachelor whom (like Shakespeare's Benedick) everyone is conspiring to press into marriage, and who in the end falls precipitately in love of his own volition. In Lovers' Vows (1798), Amelia, as strong-minded as she is outspoken, has to resist the rigorous preparations for an unwanted arranged marriage when the man she really wants to marry is her penniless private tutor, Anhalt. Elizabeth is merciless in her studies of marriage, while at the same time quite prepared to observe the contemporary conventions of comedy and pair everyone off at the end. Nevertheless, like Shakespeare, she admires intelligent and plain-spoken girls who voice their minds, and both Maria in Wives as They Were and Amelia in Lovers' Vows do just this. Maria, indeed, was thought at the time to be, either consciously or unconsciously, something of a self-portrait. Here is Amelia playing with fire when she goads the man she really loves, her tutor Anhalt, who has been sent to reconcile her to an arranged marriage with Count Cassel:

Amelia.	I will not marry.
Anhalt.	You mean to say, you will not fall in love.
Amelia.	Oh no! (Ashamed). I am in love.
Anhalt.	Are in love! (Starting). And with the Count?
Amelia.	I wish I was.
Anhalt.	Why so?
Amelia.	Because he would, perhaps, love me again.
Anhalt.	(Warmly). Who is there that would not?
Amelia.	Would you?
Anhalt.	I - I - me - I - I am out of the question.
Amelia.	No; you are the very person to whom I have put the question.
Anhalt.	What do you mean?
Amelia.	I am glad you don't understand me. I was afraid I had spoken too plain. (In confusion).
Anhalt.	Understand you! - As to that - I am not dull.
Amelia.	I know you are not - And as you have for a long time instructed me, why should not

                    I now begin to teach you?
Anhalt.   Teach me what?
Amelia.   Whatever I know, and you don't.

And here is Miss Maria Dorrillon rejecting the suit
of Bronzely:

Bronzely.   My dear Miss Dorrillon, I could not sleep
             all night, and am come thus early on
             purpose to complain of your treatment of
             me during the whole of yesterday evening.
             Not one look did you glance towards me -
             and there I sat in miserable solitude up
             in one corner, the whole time of the
             concert.
Maria.   I protest I did not see you! - and,
             stranger still! - never thought of you.
Bronzely.   You then like another better than you
             like me?
Maria.   I do.
Bronzely.   Do you tell him so?
Maria.   No.
Bronzely.   You tell him you like me best?
Maria.   Yes.
Bronzely.   Then I will believe what you say to him,
             and not what you say to me ....

Again, To Marry or not to Marry is full of bons
mots in dialogue exchanges about the relationship
of the sexes. For example, Mrs. Mortland talks
with Sir Oswin, her brother, who dislikes the idea
of marriage:

             I never made a vow against
        marriage. It was the men, I believe,
        who vowed never to ask me the question.
        Let me tell you, brother, there is a
        great deal of difference in sentiment,
        between a single man of a certain age,
        and a single woman of a certain age.
        The one does not marry, because he
        won't: - the other, because she can't.

A sentiment she echoes later in the play:

             ... at my time of life, I feel for
        every man the same disregard, the men
        all felt for me in my younger days.

Or there is Hester, in one of her sharp exchanges

with Sir Oswin:

Hester.	Am I artful? If you say so, I suppose I am; but, indeed, I did not know it.
Sir Oswin.	Were not those arts, by which you deceived two lovers?
Hester.	O! lovers! Yes, I have made fools of two lovers. But I had a right to do so - for they wanted to make a fool of me.
Sir Oswin.	How so?
Hester.	Why, Mrs. Ashdale, my guardian's wife, and all the elderly ladies, that visited her, constantly said to me, 'Hester, never mind what the men say; they are deceitful, and always speak falsehood to young women.' So, I put no trust in them, nor they, I hope in me.
Sir Oswin.	One honourable man was on the point of marrying you, when you ran away.
Hester.	I thought it was better to run away before marriage, than after.
Sir Oswin.	But you broke your promise.
Hester.	Not my marriage promise - for that I am resolved to keep, marry when I will: which makes me so afraid of giving it.

Finally, there is Lady Susan Courtly:

> The favourite lover of a woman of fashion, Mr. Willowear, has the same prerogative as a king; he never dies - there's always an immediate successor.

There may be satire but there is no negative cynicism in Elizabeth's plays. In the end, her position became that of the liberal humanitarian of the period, though with touches here and there of contemporary indulgence in sentimentality. That she abominates tyranny in any form is clear in such plays as A Case of Conscience (1800-01) in which the ill-motivated Marquis gradually has his judgment restored in favor of his ill-used wife and son (as does the equally unjust Baron in Lovers' Vows), and in her play involving the theme of prison reform, Such Things Are (1787), though the tyrant Sultan has to be revealed as a Christian in the end and repent his ways. The manipulative lawyer, Blackman, is exposed at the end of Next Door Neighbours (1791). Injustice is forced to confront itself alike in public as in private matters, so that in Wise Man of the East (1799) it is not only the would-be seducer Clarensforth who is brought around to mend his ways, but also the older generation in the Quaker Starch family, whose hypocritical disapproval of their daughter Rachel's love for the young Ensign has to be unconditionally withdrawn.

The marked influence of Jacobinism in Elizabeth's plays is, apart from two, the unperformed and suppressed tragedy, The Massacre (1792) and Such Things Are (1787), in effect non-existent. Gary Kelly in his book, The English Jacobin Novel, sees her rather as 'the natural interpreter of Kotzebue for English theatre audiences,'[36] Kotzebue being a romantic liberal. Kelly then goes on to state, rightly, that in spite of its title, The Child of Nature (1788) 'had little connection with the ideas of Rousseau or Voltaire.' Nevertheless she was undoubtedly held to be 'tainted,' since as late as 1800 she was condemned as 'the scavenger of democracy,' while in 1814 Jane Austen uses Lovers' Vows, Elizabeth's adaptation of Kotzebue's Child of Love, as a subject of dispute in Mansfield Park, though largely because of its overindulgent moral outlook.[37] As for The Massacre – the odd play out in Elizabeth's repertoire – this was the outcome of the September massacres in France, which Elizabeth chose to parallel with those of St. Bartholomew's Day. She withdrew the printed edition of this play upon the advice of her friends who had their ear to the ground.

Of Such Things Are, Kelly comments:

> The social and moral satire found in the pages of Nature and Art was not much different from that to be found in many of her popular 'humanitarian comedies' of the 1780s and '90s .... As early as 1787 she had displayed her own peculiar blend of satire and sentiment in a play based at once on the trial of Warren Hastings and on the work of Howard the prison reformer .... Even the title of the play, Such Things Are, was a harbinger of such later titles as Man as He Is and Things as They Are .... The play also anticipates a favourite theme

of English Jacobin novels of the next decade, the reconciling and ennobling power of love and sympathy - what the Jacobin philosophers called philanthropy .... The moral of the play is not far from Godwin's argument, expressed six years later in Political Justice, that tyranny corrupts a whole nation and spreads itself to every level of society.[38]

Kelly then points out the timeliness of the play in relation to the successive charges alleged against Warren Hastings in the House of Commons 1786-87 by Burke, Fox and finally (on 7 February 1787) by Sheridan in a memorable speech lasting some six hours.[39] Such Things Are was presented by Harris at Covent Garden on 10 February, with great success.

The only other plays to reveal a Jacobinical touch were Next Door Neighbours (1791) and Everyone has His Fault (1793). For comment on Next Door Neighbours Kelly cites Boaden (whom he normally regards as either unperceptive in political matters, or concerned to clear Elizabeth of any such unpleasant implications), commenting on the parallels the play offers to Nature and Art:

The interest seems to have struck the author as capable of far greater expansion, and she accordingly remembered the filial piety and honour of Henry Wilford, ready to accept a prison to release his father, when, in Nature and Art, she sends the Henry of her novel to the coast of Africa, to perish, or redeem his father. The heartless profligacy of Splendorville is remembered also in the Bishop's son, who, as a judge, passes sentence of death on the victim of his early lust; and Eleanor, however slightly, lends some few points of interest to her (i.e., Mrs. Inchbald's) Rebecca and Agnes. The turns of opposition in the dialogue, appear reflected, too, in the conversations which so abound in the romance; and we could easily show their almost immediate proximity to each other.[40]

Everyone has His Fault (produced January 1793) had reference to the newly-formed Association for Preserving Liberty and Property against Republicans and Levellers, and, says Kelly, 'immediately drew down the fire of a Government paper founded expressly to denounce sedition.' The play, however, was very successful, and its sale in published form, according to Boaden, 'immense.' But by 1794, the year of the Treason Trials, Elizabeth was concentrating on revising her Satire upon the Times (which had so shocked Hardinge) in the form of Nature and Art. She wrote to Godwin in the spring of 1794:

> And there (said I to myself as I folded up the volumes) how pleased Mr. Godwin will be at my making the King so avaricious, and there (said I to myself) how pleased the King will be at my making him so very good at the conclusion, and when he finds that by throwing away his money he can save his drowning people he will instantly throw it all away for flannel shirts for his soldiers, and generously pardon me all I have said on equality in the book, merely for giving him a good character.
>   But, alas, Mr. Godwin did not know him in that character, and very likely he would not know himself.[41]

Hardinge had warned her, along with her friend John Taylor, both men begging her to be discreet. It may seem strange that this Catholic lady should at once admire Bonaparte and the Protestant King and Queen of Great Britain - but it would seem she admired them for rather different reasons, Bonaparte for his political stance, their Majesties for the probity of their domestic life, so unlike that of the usual run of royalty in Britain, more especially the Georges. Elizabeth was essentially an eclectic thinker and writer - taking what suited her from any of the many, diverse influences of the day, whether it be Rousseau or Godwin, Catholicism or Protestantism, monarchy or republicanism, sentimental humanism or revolution. Her concept of liberal education owed much to Emile, but she by no means conforms to all that Rousseau's fable suggests. She valued her friends, revolutionary, liberal or conservative alike, accepting them as advisers but never becoming their uncritical disciple.

It goes without saying, therefore, that she took herself and her evolving values very seriously; her serious comedies are, therefore, on the sentimental side, but without becoming mawkish. Her natural wit and her brusque commonsense prevented that. She accepted the contemporary convention of the 'sentimental comedy of manners' without, again, becoming its slavish practitioner. Allardyce Nicoll, one of England's greatest historians of the drama, claims that although her work reflects the sentimental social consciousness of Continental dramatists like Kotzebue, she also remains well within the national tradition based on the style set by Jonson and Congreve:

> Many of her characters are 'humours,' while in I'll Tell You What the domestic relations of Major Cyprus and of his wife differ little from the domestic relations of Restoration husbands and wives .... The picture of Sir Robert Ramble in Everyone has his Fault, a man divorced from his wife and marrying her again, at once owes a great deal to the work of men like Etherege and Congreve, and bears a strangely modern note .... As Mrs. Inchbald advanced in life the atmosphere of Jonson came to usurp that of Congreve. I'll Tell You What contains only one artificial 'humour' in Col. D. Downright .... In Such Things Are, on the contrary, we find at least half of the dramatis personae are abstract, or at least only semi-real. There are here Sir Luke Tremor, Lord Flint, and Twineall .... In Everyone has his Fault the very basis of the play rests on the clash and interaction of the various 'humorous' types .... Even to the end, however, and particularly when we consider her portraits of women, she still preserved just that touch of life which makes almost all of her characters interesting, if not always psychological, studies .... In surveying

Mrs. Inchbald's work as a whole, we
cannot deny the fact that her plays are
as good as any of her time, and that
one, at least, I'll Tell You What,
really challenges comparison with the
comedies of Goldsmith and Sheridan. Her
sense of construction is perfect.[42]

As Park[43] points out, like Molière and
Bernard Shaw, she chose to ridicule what she
despised, using laughter to castigate immorality
and social pretensions of the time, including false
idealism, especially the hypocrisy that poverty, of
itself, ennobles, while wealth, of itself,
degrades. Though she does not go as far as Shaw's
Andrew Undershaft in Major Barbara in proclaiming
poverty to be a crime, she had the courage to show
how 'good' characters could be driven to theft in
order to preserve themselves and their dependents.

Though one is forced to agree with her
otherwise admiring critic, Bruce Robertson Park,
who feels forced to admit that she lacked genius,
she certainly possessed a high talent, with an
unusual perspicacity when it comes to delineating
human failings, which often raises farce to the
level of comedy, and elevates comedy into serious
satire. Allardyce Nicoll claims that her work is
'fresh, honest, and thoughtful.' But her
seriousness and sense of moral purpose betray her
comic sensitivity on occasion, making her appear
sentimental and even didactic. The quality of her
characterization, though often admirable, tends to
be lessened by too great an indulgence in using
types and representatives of the 'humours.'
Nevertheless, her studies of domestic life and
marriage are often no less than brilliant, and
among English women dramatists there is still no
one to touch her in the comedy of situation.

Elizabeth remains Britain's outstanding woman
dramatist. At least three of her plays are
brilliant enough to bear revival - the two lighter
plays, The Wedding Day and I'll Tell You What, and
the serious comedy, Such Things Are. Allardyce
Nicoll refers to the 'brilliance' of The Wedding
Day, the 'brightness of the dialogue,' and its
'tendencies in common' with Sheridan's The School
for Scandal; 'they present,' he writes, 'two
different fronts to the attack on sensibility.'

Second to these three outstanding plays, but well worthy of renewed attention, is the light comedy, The Married Man, and the serious comedies, Everyone has His Fault, Lovers' Vows, Next Door Neighbours and Wives as They Were and Maids as They Are. It is a notable achievement, yet, like Elizabeth's novel, Nature and Art, none of these plays has until now existed in any readily accessible modern edition.

From a Painting by Thomas Kearsley. *Engravd by Robts.*

William Godwin, Esqr.

William Godwin aged 38
Portrait by Thomas Kearsley, engraved by
P. Roberts

III

NOVELIST

The 18th century is generally acknowledged as being the first major century of the English novel. It includes the novels of writers as divergent as Defoe, Richardson, Fielding, Smollett, Sterne, Goldsmith, Mackenzie, Walpole, Godwin, Ann Radcliffe and Fanny Burney. Elizabeth's work as a novelist, published only in the 1790s, made her prominent among the many women writers of the time, in spite of her slender output compared with that of her plays. A Simple Story remains now her best known work, kept in regular print to the present time.

In one of the best of her essays, Women and Fiction, Virginia Woolf wrote with great feeling about the peculiar disabilities of the woman writer in England.[1] The history of England, she claims, has until recent times been virtually entirely the history of men written by men from an exclusively male standpoint. The daily life, preoccupations and emotions of women were largely excluded, or projected (as in the outstanding case of the women characters in the Elizabethan-Jacobean drama) as men conceived them to be. Girls seldom chose their husbands, and once married sank into a routine of child-bearing and home management which finds no place in literature until the 18th century. Virginia Woolf considers women were deprived of the living conditions, and mostly the form of education, which fitted them for the major task of conceiving and writing a fully-developed novel. Nor did they normally have the kind of life-experience out of which to create the background and vigorous activity open to the male novelist. The appropriate degree of leisure and the necessary kind of education came only in the 18th century. She also points out, significantly, that none of the four great women novelists of the 19th century in England - Jane Austen,[2] Emily Bronte, Charlotte Bronte, and George Eliot - had any children, and two of them remained unmarried. Elizabeth, whom she does not mention, was in effect in the same position - she had no children to care for, and except for a few years in the 1770s, was without a husband.

Virginia Woolf believes that a certain indignation at the way a woman was confined by domestic custom and routine may have inspired women to write the kind of literature most open to them - the novel. Its looser form of construction compared with that of either poetry or drama made it the kind of literary work that could be written in fits and starts within the framework of the domestic scene. More subtly, she says that women in the 18th century began to evolve a manner of writing that suited them and was no longer dominated by the various styles being evolved exclusively by the influential male writers from Defoe to Fielding; it was a style that responded closely to women's interests and values, a creative form that began in the 18th century but only came to fullest fruition in the characteristic novels written by women in the 20th century. Go far enough back, to Aphra Behn,[3] for instance, and there is (says Virginia Woolf) little to choose between her manner and outlook, both as a novelist and dramatist, and that of her male contemporaries.

One has to differentiate, obviously, between the conception of the early romances and that of the novel itself, a form that, evolving later, scarcely existed in England before the 18th century. Storytelling in verse and prose has an ancient lineage from epic poem to medieval romance. Heroic deeds, the activities of men believed greater, stronger, more enduring and more inspired than others, fill the earlier poems, tales and contes, their adventures and their human relationships alike fantastic and poeticised. They are beautiful abstracts of human beings. Walter Allen, in his excellent and succinct study, The English Novel, quotes Hazlitt's idea of what a novel should be, written many years after the publication of A Simple Story:

> We find here a close imitation of man and manners; we see the very web and texture of society as it really exists, and we meet it when we come into the world. If poetry has 'something more divine' in it, this savours more of

humanity. We are brought acquainted with the motives and characters of mankind, imbibe our notions of virtue and vice from practical examples.[4]

Such an understanding of the novel's place in literary experience plainly differentiated it from almost all the Elizabethan-Jacobean drama, which (for all its great understanding of human nature, culminating in that shown by Shakespeare) was at the same time raising characters, however realistically conceived, into performers in highly stylized forms of society, the courts of kings, queens, and titled intriguers far removed from the common man or woman, who make only limited appearances now and then as stylized comic characters from 'low life.'[5] The novel proper, when it finally arrived, was to eschew such a concept of human portraiture, and reflect the world as both writers and readers themselves experienced it inside and outside their homes. There are the seeds of this in Thomas Deloney's unique stories of Elizabethan apprentice life, such as Jack of Newbury (1597), or Thomas Nash's extravagant and picaresque The Unfortunate Traveller (1594) or a century later in William Dampier's A New Voyage round the World (1697).

The seeds of the more modern novel seem almost to lie in the drama, for both Bunyan (writing in the 1670s) and later Richardson use the dramatic format in The Pilgrim's Progress (1678) and Pamela (1740), with very naturalistic dialogue. Congreve had attempted to graft dramatic dialogue into what he himself termed a 'novel' in Incognita (1691), a story of intrigue, while Addison and Steele, without using the format of the novel, created splendidly conceived, realistic fictional characters such as Sir Roger de Coverley and others in their pieces for the Spectator from 1711.

We are by now well into the 18th century, in which Defoe was the initial pioneer of naturalistic story-telling with Robinson Crusoe (1719) - with its detailed, first person account of seemingly true events in which verisimilitude of character reveals an extraordinary command of cumulative detail, so remarkably displayed in the fictitious Journal of the Plague Year (1722). His portrayal of women as in <u>Moll Flanders</u> (1722) and <u>Roxana</u> (1724) - both first person narratives - is filled with the kind of worldly, naturalistic detail more familiar to the male writer than to any likely female novelist.

Defoe revealed an extraordinary capacity to reconstruct female character in the fictional form open to him early in the 18th century. As a man of the city, of the streets, he could give his women a succession of exotic environments convincing in their detail. With these precedents, Samuel Richardson (born 1689), a printer who became later Master of the Stationer's Company, found himself at the age of fifty in 1739 encouraged by a bookseller's commission to compose some kind of literary guide for young ladies in the composition of letters, and in particular a moral tale 'to instruct handsome girls' in service 'how to avoid the snares that might be laid against their virtue.' The result was the outstandingly successful <u>Pamela, or Virtue Rewarded</u> (1740), an entirely unique production, the sale of which was so great Richardson set about writing the longest novel in English, <u>Clarissa</u> (1748), little short of a million words. Both novels were composed entirely in the form of letters and responses to letters, the first person therefore dominating the narrative and giving all events an immediacy that somehow enlivens the vast mass of pages with which the reader is confronted. In the case of <u>Clarissa</u>, the story is also extraordinary, as both V. S. Pritchett and Walter Allen have alleged, for its sexual sadism.[6]

With Richardson the novel proper was fully conceived by the middle of the 18th century. There followed immediately Henry Fielding (born 1707) with <u>Joseph Andrews</u> (1742),[7] which started out merely as a satire on the supremely virtuous heroine, Pamela, by supplying her with a supremely virtuous brother, a footman whose virtue is similarly threatened. But the book became far greater than that, and was succeeded by what was probably the greatest single novel of the century, <u>The History of Tom Jones, a Foundling</u> (1749). This was followed by <u>Amelia</u> (1751), whose heroine was modeled on the character of his beloved young wife Charlotte, who died prematurely. Fielding himself died in 1754, a year after Elizabeth was born.

The characterization of the women in <u>Amelia</u>,
Mrs. Atkinson and Miss Matthews, who seduce
Amelia's husband, the weakling young officer,
William Booth, is excellent. Richardson and
Fielding had much to offer future novelists - far
more than Smollett, with his violent, gusty
exposure of the century's filth and brutality in
journalistic novels with a picaresque continuity of
action. Nor did the idiosyncratic Sterne (born
1713) offer anything to Elizabeth, with his style
of writing which he himself termed 'but a different
name for conversation' and which Walter Allen
considers anticipates the 'stream of consciousness
technique' - a pre-Freudian comic writer if ever
there was one, with his dependency on feeling,
sentiment, and sensibility (in the 18th century
implication of alertness of response to sensation,
emotion, sensitivity to people, nature and so
forth), and his predilection for indecency.[8] All
these authors died between 1754 and 1771.
Elizabeth no doubt felt more akin in spirit to
Oliver Goldsmith's over-respectable domestic novel,
<u>The Vicar of Wakefield</u> (1776), which she records
she read, and to Henry Mackenzie's <u>The Man of
Feeling</u> (1771), whose principal character is always
overwhelmed to the point of tears by the sorrows he
witnesses, and who eventually perishes through
excess of sensibility. <u>The Man of Feeling</u> was
followed by <u>Julia de Roubigné</u> in 1777, the year
Elizabeth began to write fiction herself. Closest
of all was her immediate predecessor and great
admirer, Fanny Burney, whose novel, <u>Evelina</u> (1778)
is the story of a young girl's adjustment to
society; taking an obvious cue from Richardson,
Fanny Burney wrote in letter form. Walter Allen
claims that Fanny Burney's heroine, for all her wit
and 'merciless eye for observation,' is a
conventional young girl who accepts her place in a
society dominated by masculine values, whereas the
heroine of <u>A Simple Story</u>, which he terms an
'admirable novel,' represents for the first time in
English fiction 'the attitude towards men of a
strong-willed, imperious and beautiful young woman'
beside whom Fanny Burney's Evelina is a 'priggish
mouse.'[9]

    Elizabeth's brief career as a published
novelist - confined to her two works, <u>A Simple
Story</u> (1791), which appeared when she was 37, and
<u>Nature and Art</u> (1796) - is almost entirely distinct

from that of the successful dramatist, which covered the period 1784 to 1805. Nevertheless, she had begun writing A Simple Story as early as 1777, and finished it in its initial, much shorter form by 1779, just after her husband's death. It had been turned down by the first and only publisher to whom it had been submitted. Thereafter, during the 1780s, Elizabeth concentrated more on establishing herself as actress and playwright than as novelist, though she returned from time to time to the composition of A Simple Story during the 1780s. When she finally retired from acting in 1789, she concentrated once more on the elaboration of A Simple Story, adding in effect its second part, volumes III and IV of the novel as published in 1791.

Elizabeth was in the habit of constantly testing out her work with her closer male friends. Initially her adviser had been the youthful John Philip Kemble, who can scarcely have failed to see something of himself in the character of Dorriforth, since in 1777 he had left his studies for the Catholic priesthood in order to become an actor and combine his career with that of his sister, Sarah Siddons. He must also have recognized there was much of Elizabeth's own outspoken, independent character in Miss Milner. Whatever advice she had taken or rejected came to nothing when Stockdale, the publisher, rejected the novel, essentially Volumes I and II only, in 1779.

By the time she decided to give her full attention to expanding A Simple Story to double its initial length, her advisers had become markedly different from John Philip Kemble, while she herself was no longer a provincial actress but a well-established London dramatist in her mid-thirties. The climate of the period was also different. She was working on the revisions and expansions of the book in the year of the fall of the Bastille in France. 'I was ten months, unceasingly, finishing my novel,' she recalled to William Godwin later.[10] Boaden notes that she maintained a year-by-year record of what she read; Rousseau's La nouvelle Héloise (first published in French in 1761) and Emile (1762) were evidently known to her, though not specifically mentioned by Boaden; protagonists of the new thinking in England included Holcroft and Godwin, both to grow from acquaintances into influential friends at the turn of the 1780s and 1790s.

Holcroft had read and commented upon the script of <u>A Simple Story</u>, and as Boaden points out, she was during 1789 'correcting her novel by his suggestions.' There is a note in Godwin's diary for 31 December 1790: 'It was in this year that I read and criticized the <u>Simple Story</u> in MS,' though he does not add that he actually met Elizabeth at this time, nor is her name among the lists of 'French Revolutionists' and others he met at Holcroft's and elsewhere. It would seem Godwin and Elizabeth were not to meet until 1792, by which year they were on relatively intimate terms through correspondence. (Holcroft was ten years Godwin's senior, and Elizabeth's by three years.) She was plainly at this time being drawn toward the radical movement in England, or to those volatile, questioning men who belonged to it. However, <u>A Simple Story</u> is scarcely a 'Jacobin' novel, and Godwin's principal influence would seem to have come at a later stage, and to have been primarily literary. <u>A Simple Story</u> passed through stages of meticulous revision between the second edition of March 1791 (the first edition had appeared only in February) - virtually all small emendations to clarify the style and correct small printing errors, removing minor gaucheries and 'provincialisms' of style, showing very probably Godwin's highly educated influence - through to the fourth edition of 1799 and to that of 1810, which was advertised as 'a new edition with the last corrections of the author,' the latter being in fact very slight.[11]

In her Preface to the novel (withdrawn after the second edition), Elizabeth makes what might seem an over-personal and over-depressing statement for the author of a first novel to share with her public. She wrote:

> ... the writer frankly avows, that during the time she had been writing it, she has suffered every quality and degree of weariness and lassitude, into which no other employment could have betrayed her. It has been the destiny of the writer of this Story, to be occupied throughout her life, in what

has the least suited either her inclination or capacity - with an invincible impediment in her speech, it was her lot for thirteen years to gain a subsistence by public speaking - and, with the utmost detestation to the fatigue of inventing, a constitution suffering under a sedentary life, and an education confined to the narrow boundaries prescribed her sex, it has been her fate to devote a tedious seven years to the unremitting labour of literary productions - whilst a taste for authors of the first rank has been an additional punishment, forbidding her one moment of those self-approving reflections which are assuredly due to the industrious.

She then goes on to point out that had not necessity driven her to it, she might never have accomplished the task of finishing the novel in its new and revised form. This reveals how important money was to her (it was the root of her independence from men and marriage) as well as the care she had for the dependence of others upon her - especially members of her family.

A Simple Story is more strikingly autobiographical than in any way 'revolutionary,' though it appears to have incorporated something of the newer thinking on the education of women; since she had received no formal education herself, and was now increasingly in touch with men of Godwin's intellectual stature, Elizabeth was conscious of her lack of literary polish, as the intensive, and immediate revisions of the March 1791 edition reveal. Although the primary works by fellow women writers and thinkers on female education were to come later during the 1790s (Mary Wollstonecraft's A Vindication of the Rights of Woman, 1792; Maria Edgeworth's Practical Education, 1798; Hannah More's Strictures on the Modern System of Female Education, 1799), Rousseau had sown the seed in good time to influence Elizabeth.

A Simple Story is for this and many other reasons an important novel in its time. It is by no means as simple as its title implies. Miss Milner, a girl of Protestant upbringing, is at the

68

age of eighteen, on the sudden death of her father, placed under the guardianship of Mr. Dorriforth, a young Catholic priest of noble family and impeccable character, whose household in London she is brought to join. He has rooms in the residence of the elderly Mrs. Horton, whose niece, Miss Woodley, aged 30 and a spinster, acts as her companion and confidante. Miss Milner's somewhat worldly disposition and sharp tongue soon excite criticism within this relatively austere household, especially since Dorriforth is very much under the influence of the Rev. Sandford, his stern and devout Catholic tutor. Dorriforth decides to remove his ward to a small country estate he has inherited, away from the pleasures and temptations of London, and especially from the attentions of the libertine Lord Frederick while he himself can easily be a frequent visitor to his cousin, Lord Elmwood's estate nearby, so keeping an eye on her. Present too is another young lady, Miss Fenton, as compliant and 'good' as Miss Milner is headstrong and willful. Miss Fenton is in fact being groomed to be the Earl of Elmwood's bride.

Unfortunately, Lord Frederick also has an estate nearby, and persists in his pursuit of Miss Milner, who finds him very attractive. A climax comes when, having been commanded by Dorriforth to have no further contact with Lord Frederick, Miss Milner disobeys. It is evident by now that Dorriforth's resentment is the result of a dawning jealousy, and when by accident they all meet, Dorriforth heatedly strikes Lord Frederick. The outcome is a duel, in which Dorriforth is only slightly wounded. Miss Milner's head is in a whirl; having openly declared her love for Lord Frederick, she confesses to her confidante, Miss Woodley, that she is secretly in love with Dorriforth, whom she has informed that her affection for Lord Frederick is not of a kind that would inspire her to marry him! Miss Woodley is not only aghast, but confounded by all this. All she recommends is that Miss Milner be separated from her guardian and, accordingly, she is sent to pay a prolonged visit with an elderly relative, Lady Luneham, who lives near Bath.

During this period of 'exile,' the young Lord Elmwood dies, leaving Dorriforth the inheritor of the title, and facing him with totally changed circumstances. Miss Milner languishes in her provincial isolation; she falls ill, whereupon the devoted Miss Woodley and the new Lord Elmwood rush to Bath to sustain her. They decide to bring her back to London. Lord Elmwood is released by the Vatican from his vows to the priesthood, since it is regarded as important to the status of Catholicism in Protestant England that Catholic noblemen marry and maintain their title by establishing heirs.

The new threat to Miss Milner's well-being is that the all-perfect Miss Fenton, having lost the first Lord Elmwood as future husband, appears well placed to secure the second. It is from Miss Woodley that Elmwood learns for the first time, directly, that his ward is in love with him, and a period of acute embarrassment in their relationship ensues, exacerbated by Sandford's continual and uncharitable exposure of Miss Milner's many faults, which he maintains to her face. But Lord Elmwood has also revealed an uncharitable side to his nature in his persistent rejection of any association with his nephew, a boy who has done nothing to offend him, and whose cause Miss Milner adopts successfully. Meanwhile, she has become Elmwood's affianced future wife. However, she insists on going to a masquerade despite Elmwood's total prohibition, acting still as her guardian. They have a final confrontation when she returns very late from her 'dissipation'; the engagement is broken off by him, and she receives shortly after this a letter confirming this. He is to go to Venice; but by an extraordinary volte-face, Elmwood cannot bring himself to leave her, and Sandford himself, accepting the inevitable manfully, unites them in Catholic wedlock, which is then followed next day (as the law requires) by a Protestant ceremony.[12]

Nevertheless, there is a sinister omen, for the ring Lord Elmwood in his haste slips upon his bride's finger turns out to be not a wedding-ring but a mourning-ring.

Boaden indicates that the original novel stopped at this point, no doubt with every indication of happiness for this unusual and, one would have thought, ill-matched couple. The omen of the ring reads like an intrusive addition, clumsily tacked on as a bridge to lead us into the third and fourth volumes which double the length of the work in the form of a second part that begins seventeen years later.[13]

So, it is the mourning-ring that indicates there is a rough future ahead for the Elmwood marriage. The marriage has in fact failed long before the story is taken up again. Lord Frederick has become Lady Elmwood's lover, and has been killed by Elmwood in a second duel. Sick and separated from her husband, Lady Elmwood has given birth to a single child, Elmwood's daughter, Matilda. The story resumes when exiled north to a border territory with the ever-faithful Miss Woodley she finally dies, watched over by Sandford and embracing her beloved daughter. Matilda, aged fifteen, and Miss Woodley are left in the care of Sandford (now reformed into a kindly character). Sandford in turn is dependent on Lord Elmwood, and takes this autocratic nobleman a letter of petition. Elmwood is not entirely unmoved by his daughter's situation, but vows never to lay eyes upon her.[14] He fears that she will remind him of his once-loved wife when she too was young. Given that she is kept in retirement from his sight, she and Miss Woodley are permitted to live at Elmwood Castle, which he seldom visits.

Matilda, now seventeen, and 'good' as her mother was once willful and 'bad,' longs for the affection of her father. She, Miss Woodley and Sandford (now a closely aligned group) resent the affection Elmwood lavishes on his once-rejected nephew, Rushbrook, whom he has now adopted and made his heir. Although at first Rushbrook's character is somewhat maligned, he proves when he arrives at the Castle with Elmwood to be very sympathetic. Elmwood, meanwhile, treats Miss Woodley with courtesy, but refuses to raise his total ban on any contact with his daughter; however, gradually Rushbrook and Matilda are drawn to each other, meeting as they do on occasion. When Rushbrook and Elmwood are gone away again, a Viscount Margrave, described as 'a rustic Baron,' contemplates securing Matilda in matrimony. Before he can nerve himself to undertake his campaign, Rushbrook, who has been ill, returns to the Castle. In a dramatic interchange with Sandford, he challenges the latter's hatred of him as Elmwood's heir. But

Matilda, determined to overcome her father's prejudice, meets him by accident. She faints into his arms, and the moment is one of great emotion for him in recollection of the love he had once felt for her mother. As a result, he leaves the Castle, and the news reaches Rushbrook that Matilda and Miss Woodley are to be sent away. In despair, he admits his love for Matilda to her father, and Sandford has to intervene to prevent Elmwood disowning and banishing Rushbrook, who manages to maintain his contact with Matilda. Margrave, however, carries out a plan to abduct the unprotected Matilda by force. When Elmwood learns of this, he rushes to her rescue. Reconciled at last and able to reveal his suppressed affection, he takes his daughter to live with him in London, and in time consents to her marriage to Rushbrook, who remains his heir.

A Simple Story has been called the first English Catholic novel - that is a novel in which several of the protagonists are Catholics, except for the heroine, Miss Milner. 'Her principal character, the Roman Catholic lord, is perfectly new,' was the comment made by the reviewer in The Gentleman's Magazine, and in quoting it J.M.S. Tompkins, in his Introduction to the novel in the Oxford English Novels series, is at pains to point out Elizabeth's acumen in her timing, since the English were alert to the easing of the position of Catholics in their society. The First Catholic Relief Act of 1778 enabled Catholics to purchase and inherit land, while Catholic priests were no longer subject to prosecution through common informers. The anti-Catholic Gordon Riots in 1780 in London were a step back, and coincided with the refusal of the first version of the novel by Stockdale.[15] However, in the period 1791-95 - the period during which A Simple Story ran through three editions - the Second Catholic Relief Act, sponsored by William Pitt the Younger, legalized the public celebration of Mass and allowed Catholics a freer position in practicing professions, provided they took an oath of loyalty.

A principal critic of Elizabeth Inchbald's work who writes from the Catholic standpoint, William McKee in Elizabeth Inchbald: Novelist (1935), says of her that 'although she was at times a careless Catholic, she was never a bad one.' He continues that in <u>A Simple Story</u>, 'when religion is treated positively, there is evidence that she was well-informed upon Catholic practices of the time; but there is also evidence that she had little feeling for Catholic life.' Miss Milner's father, it is noted in <u>A Simple Story</u>, was a Catholic, but her mother was a Protestant, and the arrangement between them (common at that time and indeed since) was for the sons of such a mixed marriage to be brought up Catholics, and the daughters Protestant; although the Church itself did not sanction this, it had (it would seem) to turn a blind eye to the practice in such solidly Protestant strongholds as Britain and certain states in Germany. Priests, in other words, gave 'passive assistance' at such marriages, but trouble frequently arose from this, as in the case of Miss Milner. Dorriforth, the gentleman priest, never officiates at a service (however clandestine) in <u>A Simple Story</u>, or seems to observe the rites of his faith, nor indeed does the strict mentor, Sandford, who talks all the time more like a Calvinist pastor than a Catholic priest. Both Dorriforth and Sandford are commonly addressed as 'Mr. Dorriforth' and 'Mr. Sandford,' normal for Catholic priests in public, outside clandestine Catholic circles. In short, there is little debate about, and certainly no propaganda for, the survival of Catholicism in England. There is, however, as we shall see, a far more marked comment on the education of women.

It must be kept in mind that the two periods of intense labor on <u>A Simple Story</u>, which we saw Elizabeth began in outline in 1777, was in 1779 after the death of her husband in August, and again in 1789 after her retirement from acting. For her distinct contribution to what has been termed the dramatic and psychological novel, her work has to be seen not only in the literary perspective of the period in which she was writing, but also alongside the achievements of other contemporary women novelists. Few had, in fact, published contemporary-styled fiction before her. The most notable was Fanny Burney, whose <u>Evelina</u> appeared anonymously in 1778, and her <u>Cecilia</u> in 1782. McKee, in his study of Elizabeth's novels, considers the influence of Fanny Burney's <u>Evelina</u> to be slight, especially as the first draft of the book was finished before <u>Evelina</u> was published. Other notable women writers were to publish after

A Simple Story had appeared; in any case, Ann Radcliffe's most important 'Gothic' work, The Mysteries of Udolpho, appeared in 1794, and had little in common with Elizabeth's work, while Maria Edgeworth's first novel proper, Castle Rackrent, with its realistic study of Irish life, did not appear until 1800. Ahead of Elizabeth, as of all of them, was of course to be Jane Austen (1775-1817), who had already begun in the 1790s to write her masterpieces of domestic fiction in the seclusion of her father's vicarage in Hampshire, but who was not to start publishing her work until Sense and Sensibility appeared anonymously in 1811. Twenty-two years junior to Elizabeth, she belonged to the next generation of female observers of female character, the same generation in years as Lamb (born the same year as Jane Austen, 1775), Coleridge (born 1772), Hazlitt (born 1778) and Wordsworth (born 1770). Byron, Shelley and Keats were still small children during the period Elizabeth was publishing her two novels.[16]

Ever since A Simple Story was published, from the time of those who knew Elizabeth and Kemble personally to succeeding generations of commentators, certain resemblances between them and the characters of Miss Milner and Dorriforth were immediately apparent. Boaden was not slow to point out what similarities there were. Though Kemble had begun his training for the Catholic priesthood and subsequently lost his vocation and become an actor, he had nevertheless resisted the powerful attraction he had at first felt for Elizabeth, as she for him. Perhaps the wisest comment on this matter is that of the modern scholar, J.M.S. Tompkins, who in his introduction to the Oxford University Press edition of A Simple Story makes the point that Dorriforth is more like a performance by Kemble, the mature actor, than the man in private life. The gentler Dorriforth of the first part of the novel might correspond in some measure to the younger Kemble, but the remote and intransigent father of the second part would correspond best to Kemble playing, for example, Coriolanus. Kemble, Elizabeth was to remark in later years, was never effective as the simple lover, only the lover torn by the grander passions.[17] Had the character of Dorriforth been, therefore, a dramatic role, Kemble would have been well fitted to interpret him. Here is Dorriforth as

Elizabeth portrays him in his first phase:

His figure was tall and elegant,
but his face, except a pair of dark
bright eyes, a set of white teeth, and a
graceful fall in his clerical curls of
dark brown hair, had not one feature to
excite admiration - he possessed
notwithstanding such a gleam of
sensibility diffused over each, that
many people mistook his face for
handsome, and all were more or less
attracted by it - in a word, the charm
that is here meant to be described is a
countenance - on his countenance you
beheld the feelings of his heart - saw
all its inmost workings - the quick
pulses that beat with hope and fear, or
the placid ones that were stationary
with patient resignation. On this
countenance his thoughts were pictured,
and as his mind was enriched with every
virtue that could make it valuable, so
was his honest face adorned with every
emblem of those virtues - and they not
only gave a lustre to his aspect, but
added a harmonious sound to all he
uttered; it was persuasive, it was
perfect eloquence, whilst in his looks
you beheld his thoughts moving with his
lips, and ever coinciding with what he
said.[18]

Such a portrait seems to have been drawn from
life. But here is the later Dorriforth, as
described by the priest Sandford, a picture which
has an almost Gothic quality:

'I believe I am grown afraid of
your father. - His temper is a great
deal altered from what it once was - he
exalts his voice, and uses harsh
expressions upon the least provocation -
his eyes flash lightning, and his face
is distorted with anger on the slightest
motives - he turns away his old servants
at a moment's warning, and no concession
can make their peace. - In a word, I am
more at ease when I am away from him -
and I really believe,' added he with a

smile, but with a tear at the same time,
'I really believe I am more afraid of
him in my age, than he was of me when he
was a boy.'[19]

The description of Miss Milner (she is never
known by her first name, but inter-familial use of
formal terms of address was common in the 18th
century) is possibly close to Elizabeth's concept
of herself as a young girl at the time of her
escape to London, though both the circumstances and
the economic levels are markedly different in spite
of the fact that both girls were conscious of
themselves as on their own and having to stand up
for themselves and establish a certain independence:

From her infancy she had been
indulged in all her wishes to the
extreme of folly, and habitually started
at the unpleasant voice of control - she
was beautiful, she had been too
frequently told the high value of that
beauty, and thought those moments passed
in wasteful idleness during which she
was not gaining some new conquest - she
had besides a quick sensibility, which
too frequently discovered itself in the
immediate resentment of injury or
neglect - she had acquired also the
dangerous character of a wit; but to
which she had no real pretensions,
although the most discerning critic,
hearing her converse, might fall into
this mistake. - Her replies had all the
effect of repartee, not because she
possessed those qualities which can
properly be called wit, but that what
she said was spoken with an energy, an
instantaneous and powerful perception of
what she said, joined with a real or
well-counterfeited simplicity, a quick
turn of the eye, and an arch smile of
the countenance. - Her words were but
the words of others, and, like those of
others, put into common sentences; but
the delivery made them pass for wit, as
grace in an ill proportioned figure,
will often make it pass for symmetry.[20]

Her beauty has certainly excited consternation even

before she has set foot in Mrs. Horton's watchful, censorious, Catholic household: Dorriforth gets his information from Lady Evans, a friend of Mrs. Horton:

'Dear Mr. Dorriforth, do not ask me any thing about the lady - when I saw her she was very young; though indeed that is but three months ago, and she can't be much older now.'
'She is eighteen,' answered Dorriforth, colouring with regret at the doubts her ladyship had increased, but not inspired.
'And she is very beautiful, that I can assure you,' replied her ladyship.
'Which I call no qualification,' said Dorriforth, rising from his seat in evident uneasiness.
'But where there is nothing else,' returned Lady Evans, 'let me tell you, beauty is something.'
'Much worse than nothing, in my opinion,' returned Dorriforth.
'But now, Mr. Dorriforth, do not from what I have said, frighten yourself, and imagine the young lady worse than she really is - all I know of her, is merely, that she's a young, idle, indiscreet, giddy girl, with half a dozen lovers in her suite; some coxcombs, some men of gallantry, some single, and some married.'
Dorriforth started. - 'For the first time in my life,' cried he with a manly sorrow, 'I wish I had never known her father.'[21]

Miss Milner meets with her sternest experience of rebuke in the person of Dorriforth's mentor and former tutor, Mr. (Father) Sandford:

Mr. Sandford perfectly knew how to work upon the passions of all human nature, but yet had the conscience not to 'draw all hearts towards him.' - There were of mankind, those, whose hate he thought not unworthy his holy labour; and in that, he was more rapid in his success than even in procuring esteem. In this enterprize he succeeded with Miss Milner, even beyond his most sanguine wish.

She had been educated at an English boarding school, and had no idea of the superior, and subordinate state of characters in a foreign seminary - besides, as a woman, she was privileged to say any thing she pleased; and as a beautiful woman, she had a right to expect whatever she pleased to say, should be admired.

Sandford knew the hearts of women, as well as those of men, notwithstanding he had passed but little of his time in their society - he saw Miss Milner's heart at the first view of her person; and beholding in that little circumference a weight of folly he wished to see eradicated, he began to toil in the vineyard, eager to draw upon him her detestation, in the hope he could also make her abominate herself. The mortifications of slight he was expert in, and being a man of talents, such as all companies, especially those Miss Milner often frequented, looked on with respect, he did not begin by wasting that reverence so highly valued upon ineffectual remonstrances, of which he could foresee the reception, but awakened the attention of the lady solely by his neglect of her. He spoke of her in her presence as of an indifferent person; sometimes forgot to name her when the subject required it; and then would ask her pardon and say he 'did not recollect her,' with such seeming sorrow for his fault, she could not think the offence intended, and of course felt the affront much more severely ....

This behaviour of Mr. Sandford's had its desired effect; it humbled Miss Milner in her own opinion, more than a thousand sermons would have done preached on the vanity of youth and

beauty. She felt an inward nothingness
she never knew before, and had been
cured of all her pride, had she not
possessed a degree of spirit beyond the
generality of her sex, and such as even
Mr. Sandford with all his penetration
did not expect.[22]

When the two contrary characters of the
handsome young priest and his willful charge meet
in direct confrontation, Elizabeth's dramatic
instincts (enlivened, no doubt, by numerous
memories of early differences with the youthful
Kemble) take over, and the dialogue bristles. Miss
Milner is planning to attend an assembly which
Dorriforth, as her guardian, has expressly
forbidden her to do. What follows is a splendid
example of Elizabeth's command both of a detailed
psychological inter-reaction of a group of people
and a theatrical control of action. It is just
like a scene from a play.

Just as dinner was removed, her
footman delivered a message - to her
from her milliner concerning a new dress
for the evening - the present evening
particularly marked.- Dorriforth looked
astonished.

'I thought, Miss Milner, you gave
me your word you would pass this evening
at home?'

'I mistook then - for I had before
given my word I should pass it abroad.'

'Indeed?' cried he.

'Yes, indeed;' returned she, 'and I
believe it is right I should keep my
first promise; is it not?'

'The promise you gave me then, you
do not think of any consequence.'

'Yes, certainly; if you do.'

'I do.'

'And mean, perhaps to make it of

much more consequence than it deserves, by being offended.'

'Whether or not, I am offended - you shall find I am.' And he looked so.

She caught his piercing, steadfast eye - her's were immediately cast down; and she trembled - either with shame or with resentment.

Mrs. Horton rose from her seat - moved the decanters and the fruit round the table - stirred the fire - and came back to her seat again, before another word was uttered. - Nor had this good woman's officious labours taken the least from the awkwardness of the silence, which as soon as the bustle she had made was over, returned in its full force.

At last, Miss Milner rising with alacrity, was preparing to go out of the room, when Dorriforth raised his voice, and in a tone of authority said,

'Miss Milner, you shall not leave the house this evening.'

'Sir?' - she exclaimed with a kind of doubt of what she had heard - a surprise, which fixed her hand on the door she had half opened, but which now she shewed herself irresolute whether to open wide in defiance, or to shut submissive.- Before she could resolve, Dorriforth arose from his seat, and said with a degree of force and warmth she had never heard him speak with before.

'I command you to stay at home this evening.'

And he walked immediately out of the apartment by the opposite door.- Her hand fell motionless from that she held - she appeared motionless herself for some time;- till Mrs. Horton, 'beseeching her not to be uneasy at the treatment she had received,' caused a flood of tears to flow, and her bosom to heave as if her heart was breaking.

Miss Woodley would have said something to comfort her, but she had caught the infection and could not utter a word - not from any real cause of grief did this lady weep; but there was a magnetic quality in tears, which always drew forth her's.

Mrs. Horton secretly enjoyed this scene, although the real well meaning of her heart, and ease of her conscience, did not tell her so - she, however, declared she had 'long prognosticated it would come to this;' and she 'now only thanked heaven it was no worse.'

'What would you have worse, madam?' cried Miss Milner, 'am not I disappointed of the ball?'

'You don't mean to go then?' said Mrs. Horton; 'I commend your prudence; and I dare say it is more than your guardian gives you credit for.'

'Do you think I would go,' answered Miss Milner, with an earnestness that for a time suppressed her tears, 'in contradiction to his will?'

'It is not the first time, I believe, you have acted contrary to that, Miss Milner,' returned Mrs. Horton, and affected a tenderness of voice, to soften the harshness of her words.

'If that is the case, madam,' replied Miss Milner, 'I see nothing that should prevent me now.' And she flung out of the room as if she had resolved to disobey him.- This alarmed poor Miss Woodley.

'Dear Aunt,' she cried to Mrs. Horton, 'follow and prevail upon Miss

Milner to give up her design; she means to go to the ball in opposition to her guardian's will.'

'Then,' cried Mrs. Horton, 'I'll not be an instrument in deterring her - if she does, it may be for the best; it may give Mr. Dorriforth a clearer knowledge what means are proper to use, to convert her from evil.'

'But, dear madam, she must be prevented the evil of disobedience; and as you tempted, you will be the most likely to dissuade her - but if you will not, I must endeavour.'

Miss Woodley was leaving the room to perform this good design, when Mrs. Horton, in humble imitation of the example given her by Dorriforth, cried,

'Niece, I command you not to stir out of this room, this evening.'

Miss Woodley obediently sat down - and though her thoughts and heart were in the chamber with her friend, she never shewed by one impertinent word, or by one line of her face, the restraint she suffered.[23]

The impulsive love of Miss Milner for Dorriforth comes to the surface in a dramatic scene of sudden admission of this affection to Miss Woodley, following shortly upon the news of the duel between Dorriforth and Lord Frederick; to prevent any injury to Dorriforth she is ready to admit she has no lasting love for Lord Frederick in spite of her willful and wayward behavior with him, born subconsciously of her desire to rouse Dorriforth's jealousy:

'Do you suppose I <u>can</u> love him?- Oh fly, Miss Woodley, and prevent my guardian from telling him such an untruth.'

'What do you mean?' repeated Miss Woodley; 'I protest you frighten me:'-

and this inconsistency in the behaviour of Miss Milner, really appeared as if her senses had been deranged.

'Only fly,' resumed she, 'and prevent the inevitable ill consequence which must ensue from Lord Frederick's being told this falsehood.- It will involve us all in greater disquietude than we suffer at present.'

'Than what has influenced you, my dear Miss Milner?'-

'That which impels my every action,' returned she; 'an unsurmountable instinct - a fatality, that will ever render me the most miserable of human beings; and yet you, even you, my dear Miss Woodley, will not pity me.'

Miss Woodley pressed her close in her arms, and vowed, 'That while she was unhappy, from whatever cause, she still would pity her.'

'Go to Mr. Dorriforth then, and prevent him from imposing upon Lord Frederick.'

'But that imposition is the only means to prevent the duel,' replied Miss Woodley. 'The moment I have told him you have no regard for his lordship, he will no longer refuse to fight with him.'

'Then at all events I am undone,' exclaimed Miss Milner, 'for the duel is horrible, even beyond every thing else.'

'How so?' returned Miss Woodley, 'since you have declared you do not care for Lord Frederick.'

'But are you so blind,' returned Miss Milner with a degree of madness in her looks, 'to believe I do not care for Mr. Dorriforth? Oh, Miss Woodley! I love him with all the passion of a mistress, and with all the tenderness of a wife.'

Miss Woodley at this sentence sat down - it was on a chair that was close to her - her feet could not have taken her to any other.- She trembled - she was white as ashes, and deprived of speech. Miss Milner, taking her by the hand, said,

'I know what you feel - I know what you think of me - and how much you hate and despise me.- But Heaven is witness to all my struggles - nor would I, even to myself, acknowledge the shameless prepossession, till forced by a sense of his danger' -

'Silence,' cried Miss Woodley, struck with horror.

'And even now,' resumed Miss Milner, 'have I not concealed it from all but you, by plunging myself into a new difficulty, from whence I know not how I shall be extricated?- And do I entertain a hope? No, Miss Woodley, nor ever will.- But suffer me to own my folly to you - to entreat your soothing friendship to free me from my weakness.- And, oh! give me your friendly advice to deliver me from the difficulties which surround me.'[24]

The impulse of such love as Miss Milner has for Dorriforth is carefully described before she goes (after the duel) to see Dorriforth alone:

Let not the reader, nevertheless imagine, there was in that ardent expectation, one idea which the most spotless mind, in love, might not have indulged without reproach. - Sincere love, (at least among the delicate of the female sex) is often gratified by that degree of enjoyment, or rather forbearance, which would be torture in the pursuit of any other passion - real, delicate, and restrained love, like that

84

of Miss Milner's was indulged in the sight of the object only; and having bounded her wishes by her hopes, the height of her happiness was limited to a conversation in which no other but themselves partook a part.[25]

Nevertheless, once Dorriforth is freed from his vows and can contemplate marriage with his ward, this does not prevent Miss Milner provoking him dangerously at a very time when she has learnt that he disapproves of her extravagances and even of the frivolous company she continues to keep, and could indeed break off his engagement to her:

Instead of shuddering with fear at the menace Lord Elmwood had uttered, she boldly said, she 'Dared him to perform it.' 'He durst not,' repeated she.

'Why durst not?' said Miss Woodley.

'Because he loves me too well - because his own happiness is too dear to him.'

'I believe he loves you,' replied Miss Woodley, 'and yet there is a doubt if - '

'There shall be no longer a doubt,'- cried Miss Milner, 'I'll put him to the proof.'

'For shame, my dear! you talk inconsiderately - what do you mean by proof?'

'I mean, I will do something that any prudent man ought not to forgive; and yet, with that vast share of prudence he possesses, I will force him still to yield to his love.'

'But suppose you should be disappointed, and he should not yield?' said Miss Woodley.

'Then, I have only lost a man who had no regard for me.'

'He may have a great regard for you, notwithstanding.'

'But for the love I have, and do still bear my Lord Elmwood, I will have something more than a <u>great regard</u> in return.'

'You have his love, I am sure.'

'But is it such as mine?- <u>I</u> could love <u>him</u> if he had a thousand <u>f</u>aults.- And <u>yet</u>,' said she, recollecting herself, 'and yet, I believe his being faultless, was the first cause of my passion.'[26]

While on the psychological plane Miss Milner - 'the gay, the proud, the haughty,' as Elizabeth describes her, at once as tender-hearted and sensitive as she is spirited and often intractable - seems a very completely realized character with whom her creator closely identifies; Dorriforth remains for all the care Elizabeth gives him a figure of melodrama set up to challenge her heroine to do both her worst and her best. The stern-minded priest becomes the considerate, but always critical lover in the first part of the novel, and Elizabeth is concerned to establish in him the seeds of intransigence which are to make him behave like a tyrant during most of the second part. This dichotomy is difficult to accept, and is shown in his utterly unworthy and un-Christian attitude to Harry Rushbrook, his young nephew, with whom he has refused all contact because he disapproves of his sister's marriage without his, Dorriforth's, consent as elder brother. The tender-hearted Miss Milner challenges providence yet again by introducing the child into Dorriforth's presence without his knowing who the boy actually is. The incident that follows shows the grave fault that lies in the saintly Dorriforth's nature:

'We will not tell Mr. Dorriforth the child is his nephew, Miss Woodley, unless he should appear fond, and pleased with him, and then we may venture without any danger.'

This was agreed, and when Dorriforth entered the room just before dinner, poor Harry Rushbrook was introduced to him as the son of a lady who frequently visited there. The deception passed - Dorriforth shook hands with him, and at length highly pleased with his engaging wiles, and applicable replies, took him on his knee, and kissed him with affection. Miss Milner could scarcely restrain the joy this gave her; but unluckily, Dorriforth said soon after to the child, 'And now tell me your name.'

'Harry Rushbrook,' replied he with great force and clearness in his voice.

Dorriforth was holding him fondly round the waist as he stood with his feet upon his knees; and at this reply he did not throw him from him - but he removed his hands, which supported him, so suddenly, that the child to prevent falling on the floor, threw himself about his uncle's neck.- Miss Milner and Miss Woodley turned aside to conceal their tears. 'I had like to have been down,' cried Harry, fearing no other danger.- But his uncle took hold of each hand that had twined around him, and placed him immediately on the ground; and dinner being that instant served, he gave no greater marks of his resentment than calling for his hat, and walking instantly out of the house.

Miss Milner cried for anger; yet she did not treat with less kindness the object of this vexatious circumstance: she held him in her arms all the while she sat at table, and repeatedly said to him, (though he had not the sense to thank her) 'she would always be his friend.'[27]

In the second part of the novel, this intractable and inhumane form of rejection is transferred from Rushbrook (whom Lord Elmwood adopts and makes his heir) to Matilda, his

87

daughter. Having rejected his wife after her
adulterous relationship with Lord Frederick, he
makes provision for his 15-year-old daughter and
her faithful companion, Miss Woodley, only on
condition that he never sees her, even when they
are both under the same roof. Nevertheless,
Elizabeth has to sow the seeds of his repressed
concern for his child, and even the residue of his
feeling for his wife, as at the moment he learns of
her death:

> Lord Elmwood had so much feeling
> upon reading this, as to lay down the
> paper, and not take it up again for
> several minutes - nor did he taste his
> chocolate during this interval, but
> leaned his elbow on the table and rested
> his head upon his hand.- He then rose
> up - walked two or three times across
> the room - sat down again - took up the
> paper - and read as usual.- Nor let the
> vociferous mourner, or the perpetual
> weeper, here complain of his want of
> sensibility - but let them remember Lord
> Elmwood was a man - a man of
> understanding - of courage - of
> fortitude - with all, a man of the
> nicest feelings - and who shall say, but
> that at the time he leaned his head upon
> his hand, and rose to walk away the
> sense of what he felt, he might not feel
> as much as Lady Elmwood did in her last
> moments.[28]

The parallel confrontation between Elmwood
and Henry Rushbrook in the first section of the
novel is re-enacted with greater emotion in the
second part when by accident he finds himself face
to face with his daughter Matilda for the first
time:

> One beautiful forenoon, about
> eleven o'clock, seeing Miss Woodley
> walking on the lawn before the house,
> she hastily took her hat to join her;
> and not waiting to put it on, went
> nimbly down the great staircase with it
> hanging on her arm.- When she had
> descended a few stairs, she heard a
> footstep walking slowly up; and (from

what emotion she could not tell,) she
stopt short, half resolved to return
back.- She hesitated a single instant
which to do - then went a few steps
farther till she came to the second
landing place; when, by the sudden
winding of the staircase, - Lord Elmwood
was immediately before her!

She had felt something like
affright before she saw him - but her
reason told her she had nothing to fear,
as he was far away.- But now the
appearance of a stranger whom she had
never before seen; an air of authority
in his looks as well as in the sound of
his steps; a resemblance to the portrait
she had seen of him; a start of
astonishment which he gave on beholding
her; but above all - her _fears_ confirmed
her it was him.- She gave a scream of
terror - put out her trembling hands to
catch the balustrades on the stairs for
support - missed them - and fell
motionless into her father's arms.

He caught her, as by that impulse
he would have caught any other person
falling for want of aid.- Yet when he
found her in his arms, he still held her
there - gazed on her attentively - and
once pressed her to his bosom.

At length, trying to escape the
snare into which he had been led, he was
going to leave her on the spot where she
fell, when her eyes opened and she
uttered, 'Save me.'- Her voice unmanned
him.- His long-restrained tears now
burst forth - and seeing her relapsing
into the swoon again, he cried out
eagerly to recall her.- Her name did
not however come to his recollection -
nor any name but this - 'Miss Milner -
Dear Miss Milner.'

That sound did not awake her; and
now again he wished to leave her in this
senseless state, that not remembering
what had passed, she might escape the

punishment.[29]

The essential style in which the novel is written has caused some differences among key critics. McKee in his <u>Elizabeth Inchbald: Novelist</u> considers her style to be plain rather than elegant; Tompkins, in his Introduction to <u>A Simple Story</u> written over thirty years later in 1967 considers (as we have seen) Godwin's principal contribution had been to help her iron out small clumsinesses of prose style, since there are 'hundreds of small corrections of order, syntax and vocabulary' as between the editions of February and March 1791, representing, as he puts it, 'the care Mrs. Inchbald took to surmount the drawbacks of an imperfect education.' It must be remembered that Elizabeth's reputation as a writer was based entirely on the writing of dialogue and the structuring of plays which would be effective in the theatre. As a novelist and prose writer she was a novice, and well aware of her shortcomings which became only too apparent to her during the prolonged period of gestation and rewriting to which her novel had been subjected. Her strength lay in her knowledge of character and her command of all the nuances of dialogue in its relation to human behavior. This was what made her novel so influential in its time. If Godwin helped her to overcome any uneasiness in prose style, she taught him, and her successors among the novelists, increased concern with the detailed actuality of human nature, the inter-reaction of characters in their behavior and speech.

McKee, like Kelly in his study, <u>The English Jacobin Novel</u>, considers the break between the first and second sections of the novel justified on the grounds of literary economy. Elizabeth, he maintains, was concerned to show in the first section 'how marriage between two irreconcilable characters brings tragedy, not only upon the first but upon the second generation as well.'[30] Not to have made the decisive jump in time would have merely meant space spent detailing Lady Elmwood's final seduction at the hands of Lord Frederick, and Lord Elmwood's consequent rejection of her and the daughter (at the age of seven - Elizabeth's own age when her father had died) and the long period of separation. Nevertheless, he considers Elizabeth as a novelist far better at female characterization than at structural continuity, at creating successive scenes between the characters than at narration. The plot is held together by Dorriforth (Elmwood), Sandford and Miss Woodley, whose presences span the whole narrative, whereas Miss Milner (Lady Elmwood) disappears all but completely at the end of the first section to be replaced by her daughter (and virtual opposite in character), who, however, resembles her physically and, in the eyes of her father, quite evidently appears to be the replica of his dead wife. Sandford too becomes, as a character, the victim of the narrative's strategy - since after her marriage he becomes the supporter of the woman he had perpetually denigrated, and the close ally of Matilda and Miss Woodley throughout the second section. McKee considers Elizabeth's male characters weak - 'semi-strangers to their creator ... she treats them almost entirely from an objective point of view. She judges man by his actions; motives she leaves untouched' except for rare, 'inaccurate' analyses.[31] Even in the case of the women (Miss Milner, Miss Woodley, and later Matilda), he considers she is far better at inventing the characters than at developing them.

Kelly, writing later, considers the strength of Elizabeth's conception of character lay first of all in its semi-autobiographical nature, and that this approach was to influence Godwin and set up the trend towards greater realism in characterization, the novel reflecting Elizabeth's own experience of life and relationships with men, her feeling for them, and her desire to be admired by them. Miss Milner represents for her 'the struggle of pride against sensibility,' whereas Dorriforth has to 'reconcile his pride with his sensibility.' This is what unites the two sections of the novel, in his view. He praises her, too, for being very rarely sentimental, though often expressing sentiment as when, in the second section, Matilda impulsively kisses Miss Woodley's hand because it was the hand her father had recently held in greeting. Kelly observes that, 'Mrs. Inchbald reveals an astonishing penetration into deep psychological disturbance and its symptoms which had to wait over a century for fully scientific exposition.' 'It is indeed the finest achievement,' he adds, 'perhaps the only major achievement of Mrs. Inchbald the novelist to show' by intelligible but simple signs 'the repression and the force of powerful but natural feelings.'[32] As The Critical Review put it at the time (February 1791), 'the workings of the passions are inimitably displayed.' Indeed, A Simple Story is a study in locked-up emotion and its ultimate need for expression. As Kelly puts it, 'the severe and terrible denial of natural affection.'

This is a considerable tribute, and due, Kelly considers, to Elizabeth's willingness to introduce her own experiences, and her 'life-long involvement with men much older than herself.' He considers she projected aspects of herself into both characters - mother and daughter - and that Matilda, in particular, paralleled the circumstances of her own childhood, losing a father around the age of 7, and in consequence developing a special need for a father-figure in later life. Writing only a generation after Elizabeth herself, Hazlitt's tribute to her has its own quality of emotional involvement with her characters:

> Mrs. Inchbald's heroes or heroines ... are an essence of sentiment. Their words are composed of the warmest breath, their tears scald, their sighs stifle. Her characters seem moulded of a softer clay [than Mrs. Radcliffe's], the work of fairest hands. Miss Milner is enchanting. Dorriforth is indeed severe, and has a very stately opinion of himself, but he has spirit and passion .... The fascination of the writer's personal feelings never quits you.

And again elsewhere:

> There is the true soul of a woman breathing from what she writes, as much as if you heard her voice. It is as if Venus had written books.[33]

Kelly considers A Simple Story as a 'pre-Jacobin' novel, one to have a great influence on succeeding, more fully Jacobin fiction. McKee, taking into account the opinion of others, considers the book is not what is termed a 'purpose novel.' It is not didactic in intention. Dr.

Joughin, in his The Life and Work of Elizabeth
Inchbald (1933) agrees: 'there is very little
outright philosophy to be found in its pages.'[34]
Kelly, however, disagrees to the point of claiming
that 'in a very real sense it is a "philosophical"
novel,' and that a considerable deal of background
reading and personal thought went into the
composition of the tale. It is here that the issue
of female education comes into play, and the much
debated theories of Rousseau (to whose writing
Elizabeth had given considerable study). Kelly
points out how the lack of any real education in
Miss Milner's case affords her no standards to
guide her behavior, which in the end makes her
through vanity and boredom a victim to Lord
Frederick. She gave way 'to that impatient,
irritable disposition she had so seldom governed.'
Matilda, on the other hand, receives a sound
education and a solid code of conduct to guide
her. She does not succumb to Margrave, who has to
use physical violence to abduct her. At the end of
A Simple Story, Elizabeth follows tradition in
making a firm moral declaration about Miss Milner:

> Mr. Milner, Matilda's grandfather,
> had better have given his fortune to a
> distant branch of his family — as
> Matilda's father once meant to do - so
> he had bestowed upon his daughter
> A PROPER EDUCATION.

A conclusion no doubt inserted on the advice of
Godwin or Holcroft. Miss Milner, it will be
remembered, had received the education (that is,
social polish) considered suitable for a rich young
girl, and 'from her infancy she had been indulged
in all her wishes to the extreme of folly.'
Matilda, on the other hand, is reared with every
care by Miss Woodley and by Sandford:

> Educated in the school of
> adversity, and inured to retirement from
> her infancy ... she was fond of walking
> and riding, was accomplished in the arts
> of music and drawing ... and as a
> scholar she excelled most of her sex,
> from the great pains Sandford had taken
> with that part of her education, and the
> great abilities he possessed for the
> task.[35]

Elizabeth Inchbald and William Godwin

According to his biographer, Ford K. Brown,[36] Godwin's first contact with Elizabeth came when in 1790 he read the script of her novel for the publisher. There is no record that they actually met until 1792, though since Godwin and Holcroft were closely connected, she should have learnt from Holcroft much about him. She was to become a mamber of the 'salon' of beautiful women who circled round this commanding personality, with his splendid intellect and skeptical mind. She was three years older than he, and she undoubtedly held her own with him; indeed, the evidence seems to point that she was to influence him, at least as a writer of fiction, as he was to influence her thinking.

According to an entry in his manuscript journal, it would appear that their friendship reached a sufficiently intimate stage for Godwin to feel himself able to propose marriage to her on 16 September 1793.[37] Many of her letters to him survive from this period, and suggest some degree of mutual affection, for example in her letter to him of 3 November 1792 about her play, The Massacre:

> Sir,- There is so much tenderness mixed with the justice of your criticism, that, while I submit to the greatest part of it as unanswerable, I feel anxious to exculpate myself in those points where I believe it is in my power.
>
> You accuse me of trusting to newspapers for my authority. I have no other authority (no more, I believe, has half England) for any occurrence which I do not see: it is by newspapers that I am told that the French are at present victorious; and I have no doubt but you will allow that (in this particular, at least) they speak truth.
>
> 2ndly. There appears an inconsistency in my having said to you, 'I have no view to any public good in this piece,' and afterwards alluding to its preventing future massacres: to

this I reply that it was your hinting to me that it might do harm which gave me the first idea that it might do good.

   3rdly. I do not shrink from Labour, but I shrink from ill-health, low spirits, disappointment, and a long train of evils which attend on Laborious Literary work. I was ten months, unceasingly, finishing my novel, notwithstanding the plan (such as you saw it) was formed, and many pages written. My health suffered much during this confinement, my spirits suffered more on publication; for though many gentlemen of the first abilities have said to me things high in its favour, it never was liked by those people who are the readers and consumers of novels; and I have frequently obtained more pecuniary advantage by ten days' labour in the dramatic way than by the labour of this ten months.[38]

Their friendship survived her refusal to marry him. Undated letters from the period prior to the publication of Caleb Williams (published May, 1794), his first considerable venture into fiction, record her excited reaction to this novel:

   God bless you!

   That was the sentence I exclaimed when I had read about half a page.

   Nobody is so pleased when they find anything new as I am. I found your style different from what I have ever yet met. You come to the point (the story) at once, another excellence. I have now read as far as page 32 (I was then interrupted by a visitor) and do not retract my first sentence. I have to add to your praise that of a most minute, and yet most concise method of delineating human sensations.

   I could not resist writing this, because my heart was burthened with the desire of saying what I think and what I hope for.

My curiosity is greatly increased
by what I have read, but if you
disappoint me you shall never hear the
last of it, and instead of 'God Bless,'
I will vociferate, God ---m you.[39]

She followed this up with a second letter when she
had finished the story:

Sir,- Your first volume is far
inferior to the two last. Your second
is sublimely horrible - captivatingly
frightful.

Your third is all a great genius
can do to delight a great genius, and I
never felt myself so conscious of, or so
proud of giving proofs of a good
understanding, as in pronouncing this to
be a capital work.

It is my opinion that fine ladies,
milliners, mantua-makers, and
boarding-school girls will love to
tremble over it, and that men of taste
and judgment will admire the superior
talents, the incessant energy of mind
you have evinced.

In these two last volumes, there
does not appear to me (apt as I am to be
tired with reading novels) one tedious
line, still there are lines I wish
erased. I shudder lest for the sake of
a few sentences, (and these particularly
marked for the reader's attention by the
purport of your preface) a certain set
of people should hastily condemn the
whole work as of immoral tendency, and
rob it of a popularity which no other
failing it has could I think endanger.

This would be a great pity,
especially as these sentences are
trivial compared to those which have not
so glaring a tendency, and yet to the
eye of discernment are even more
forcible on your side of the question ...

But if I find fault it is because I have no patience that anything so near perfection should not be perfection.[40]

A further letter survives from this period relating to Elizabeth's script called <u>A Satire on the Times</u>, which she was urged to destroy on the advice of her friends:

I am infinitely obliged to you for all you have said, which amounts very nearly to all I thought.

But indeed I am too idle, and too weary of the old rule of poetical justice to treat my people, to whom I have given birth, as they deserve, or rather I feel a longing to treat them according to their deserts, and to get rid of them all by a premature death, by which I hope to surprise my ignorant reader, and to tell my informed one that I am so wise as to have as great a contempt for my own efforts as he can have.

And now I will discover to you a total want of <u>aim</u>, of <u>execution</u>, and every particle of genius belonging to a writer, in a character in this work, which from the extreme want of resemblance to the original, you have not even reproached me with the fault of not drawing accurately.

I really and soberly meant (and was in hopes every reader would be struck with the portrait) Lord Rinforth to represent his Most Gracious Majesty, George the 3rd.

I said at the comencement all Lords of Bedchambers were mirrors of the Grand Personage on whom they attended, but having Newgate before my eyes, I dressed him in some virtues, and (notwithstanding his avarice) you did not know him.

The book is now gone to Mr.

97

Hardinge. Mr. Holcroft is to have it as soon as his play is over, and though I now despair of any one finding out my meaning, yet say nothing about the matter to Mr. Holcroft, but let my want of talent be undoubted, by his opinion conforming to yours.

And there, (said I to myself as I folded up the volumes) how pleased Mr. Godwin will be at my making the King so avaricious, and there, (said I to myself) how pleased the King will be at my making him so very good at the conclusion, and when he finds that by throwing away his money he can save his drowning people he will instantly <u>throw it all away</u> for flannel shirts for his soldiers, and generously pardon me all I have said on <u>equality</u> in the book, merely for giving him a good character.

But alas, Mr. Godwin did not know him in that character, and very likely he would not know himself.[41]

Elizabeth was not without her rivals in Godwin's wide-ranging circle. He had met Mary Wollstonecraft along with Tom Paine and others on Sunday 13 November 1791, but they had at that time violently disagreed. He also in 1793 met the 'Belle of Norwich,' Amelia Alderson, whom Southey described as 'the liveliest of the lively, the gayest of the gay;' she wrote bad poetry and sympathized with the cause of reform. She admired Elizabeth, whom she met in Godwin's company, 'as pretty as ever, and much more easy and unreserved in her manner,' she thought; he also came to know another charmer of beauty and intelligence, Mrs. Mary Reveley, and they formed a close (if platonic) friendship of sufficient warmth to cause her husband some jealousy. Other women in his life were the actress, Mrs. Robinson (who had been mistress for a while of the Prince of Wales when in her early twenties), whom he was always to consider the most beautiful woman he had ever known, and the zealous novelist, Mary Hays, another republican sympathizer and champion of women's rights, all of which brought her into disrepute and encouraged her to propose marriage to Godwin later in 1795 or early in 1796, when Godwin was a celibate 40-year-old. However, the 37-year-old Mary Wollstonecraft returned disillusioned to London in 1796 after a three-year absence abroad, recently deserted by Gilbert Imlay, the American with whom she had been living.[42] She brought with her Imlay's two-year-old daughter. Godwin now formed a very different opinion of her - 'in all the world there was no woman, perhaps no being, her equal' - and in September 1796 they began very secretly to establish an intimate relationship though without the legal benefits of marriage itself, in which neither of them professed to believe. Both by now were to some degree social outcasts in London as a result of Godwin's book, <u>Political Justice</u> (1793) and Mary's <u>Rights of Woman</u> (1792). Once they knew that Mary was pregnant, they were to marry, very quietly, on 29 March 1797.

Elizabeth was profoundly upset when the marriage came to her knowledge. There was undoubtedly some incompatibility between the two women. In 1789 Mary had reviewed one of Elizabeth's plays disparagingly - 'insipid dialogue,' she wrote, 'uninteresting characters ... Childish tricks.'[43] Prior to her marriage, Mary was in the habit of calling Elizabeth, 'Mrs. Perfection' in her letters to Godwin, for even after their relationship had become intimate, Godwin and Mary lived separately, and therefore wrote constantly to each other. Jealousy is evident in Mary's remarks to Godwin in a letter of 24 August 1796: 'As you are to dine with Mrs. Perfection today, it would be dangerous not to remind you of my existence.' Indeed she reminded him she would be present in spirit, watching over his left shoulder. Nevertheless, the ladies met socially from time to time. In a letter to Godwin of 4 September, Mary said that she had even gone out with Elizabeth: 'We had less wit and more cordiality - and if I do not admire her more I love her better. A charming woman!' But Elizabeth had on this occasion spoken of Godwin with 'affection' - 'so much so,' wrote Mary, 'that I began to think you were not out in your conjecture - you know what.' Evidently, Mary suspected Elizabeth was in love with Godwin, and that Godwin was aware of it, perhaps even vain about it. It is evident that he wanted to maintain his friendship with Elizabeth after the marriage, and was saddened when this proved impossible. In his <u>Memoirs of Mary Wollstonecraft</u>, written immediately after her death and published in January 1798, Godwin plainly tried to minimize the differences that had arisen, when he wrote: 'Two of the persons, the loss of whose acquaintance Mary principally regretted upon this occasion were Mrs. Inchbald and Mrs. Siddons.'[44]

Soon after the marriage had taken place, a theatre party was to have been arranged through Elizabeth for 19 April, but on 11 April she wrote, tartly:

> I most sincerely wish you and Mrs. Godwin joy. But, assured that your joyfulness would obliterate from your memory every trifling engagement, I have entreated another person to supply your place, and perform your office in securing a box on Reynold's night. If I have done wrong, when you next marry, I will act differently.[45]

This, very naturally, upset Mary Godwin, who wrote to Miss Alderson:

> I have now to tell you that I am very sorry I prevented you from engaging a box for Mrs. Inchbald, whose conduct, I think, has been very rude. She wrote to Mr. Godwin today, saying, that, taking it for granted he had forgotten it, she had spoken to another person. 'She would not do so the next time he was married.' Nonsense! I have now to request you to set the matter right. Mrs. Inchbald may still get a box; I beg her pardon for misunderstanding the business, but Mr. G. led me into the error; or I will go into the pit.[46]

Whether Elizabeth (and for that matter her friend, Sarah Siddons) decided they no longer wanted to associate with the new Mrs. Godwin for reasons of propriety - for the marriage to Godwin had underlined the absence of any previous marriage to Imlay - or for other, more personal reasons, cannot be determined. The theatre party was not a success and it would seem that Elizabeth behaved slightingly to Mary; in her own words, she made it clear she 'resisted a longer and more familiar acquaintance.' Mary's bitter comment on the social ostracism with which she found herself faced was that it represented a 'criminal compliance with the prejudice of society.' Miss Alderson also appears to have had certain reservations, the nature of which she does not make clear. She wrote to Mrs. John Taylor:

> Mr. Godwin was much gratified by your letter ....; by the bye, he never told me whether you congratulated him on his marriage or not ....Heighho! what charming things would sublime theories be, if one could only make one's practice keep up with them; but I am convinced it is impossible .... I shall have so much to tell you in a tête-à-tête, of the Godwins, etc. - so much that a letter could not contain it or do it justice; but this will be entre nous; I love to make observations on extraordinary characters; but not to mention those observations if they be not favourable.[47]

But the Godwins retained the loyal friendship of Mary Hays, Mrs. Reveley, and Holcroft. However, on 30 August Mary's daughter was born; complications attended the birth, and by 10 September Mary was dead. Godwin, heart-broken, wrote immediately to Holcroft:

> I firmly believe that there does not exist her equal in the world. I know from experience that we were formed to make each other happy. I have not the least expectation that I can now ever know happiness again.[48]

He also wrote to Elizabeth on the day of Mary's death:

> My wife died at eight this morning. I always thought you used her ill, but I forgive you. You told me you did not know her. You have a thousand good and great qualities. She had a very deep-rooted admiration for you.

Yours, with real honour and esteem, W.
Godwin.[49]

Elizabeth's reply was a strange one, written
immediately, undated but evidently on 10
September. It is scarcely generous in either tone
or implication:

> 'I did not know her. I never
> wished to know her; as I avoid every
> female acquaintance, who has no husband,
> I avoided her. Against my desire you
> made us acquainted. With what justice I
> shunned her, your present note evinces,
> for she judged me harshly. She first
> thought I used her ill, for you would
> not. I liked her - I spoke well of
> her. Let Charlotte Smith be my witness,
> who received her character from me, such
> as I gave of her to everybody.

> 'Be comforted. You will be
> comforted. Still I feel for you at
> present. Write to me again. Say what
> you please at such a time as this; I
> will excuse and pity you.'[50]

The problem of making the appropriate
observation in the form of condolence after their
rift evidently troubled Elizabeth. The following
day, 11 September, she wrote again, still firm in
her self-defense:

> The ceremony of condolence is an
> impertinence, but if you consider mine
> superior to ceremony, you will accept it.

> I have too much humility to offer
> consolation to a mind like yours. I
> will only describe sensations which
> nearly a similar misfortune excited in
> me.

> I felt myself for a time bereft of
> every comfort the world could bestow,
> but these opinions passed away, and gave
> place to others, almost the reverse.

> I was separated from the only
> friend I had in the world, and by

circumstances so much more dreadful than those which have occurred to you, as the want of warning increases all our calamities, but yet I have lived to think with indifference of all I then suffered.

You have been a most kind husband, I am told. Rejoice, - the time <u>might</u> have come when you would have wept over her remains with compunction for cruelty to her.

While you have no self-reproaches to wound you, be pacified. Every ill falls short of that.

I lament her as a person whom you loved. I am shocked at the unexpected death of one in such apparent vigour of mind and body; but I feel no concern for any regret she endured at parting from this world, for I believe she had tact and understanding to despise it heartily. Mr. Twiss received the news with sorrow, and Mrs. Twiss shed many tears. They were not prepared, any more than myself, for the news, for they had not heard of her illness. I showed them your note to me, and if you had seen the manner in which they treated your suspicion of my influence with them (and that was certainly your only meaning), you would beg my pardon.

I shall be glad to hear of your health, and that your poor little family are well, for believe me concerned for your welfare.[51]

Godwin replied on 13 September:

I must endeavour to be understood as to the unworthy behaviour with which I charge you towards my wife. I think your shuffling behaviour about the taking places to the comedy of the 'Will,' dishonourable to you. I think your conversation with her that night at the play base, cruel, and insulting.

103

There were persons in the box who heard it, and they thought as I do. I think you know more of my wife than you are willing to acknowledge to yourself, and that you have an understanding capable of doing some small degree of justice to her merits. I think you should have had magnanimity and self-respect enough to have shewed this. I think that while the Twisses and others were sacrificing to what they were silly enough to think a proper etiquette, a person so out of all comparison their superior, as you are, should have placed her pride in acting upon better principles, and in courting and distinguishing insulted greatness and worth; I think that you chose a mean and pitiful conduct, when you might have chosen a conduct that would have done you immortal honour. You had not even their excuse. They could not (they pretended) receive her into their previous circles. You kept no circle to debase and enslave you.

I have now been full and explicit on this subject, and have done with it, I hope, for ever.

I thank you for your attempt at consolation in your letter of yesterday. It was considerate, and well-intended, although its consolations are utterly alien to my heart.[52]

Elizabeth wrote somewhat coldly about Mary's death to her friend, Mrs. Philips:

She was attended by a woman, whether from partiality or economy I can't tell - but from no affected prudery I am sure. She had a very bad time, and they at last sent for an intimate acquaintance of his, Mr. Carlisle, a man of talents. He delivered her; she thanked him, and told him he had saved her life: he left her for two hours - returned, and pronounced she must die. Still she languished three or four days. This is the account

104

I have heard from _him_; he has written to
me several times since; but they are
more like distracted lines than anything
rational.[53]

Boaden, who reproduces this letter does not give
its date, but as she says, the correspondence with
Godwin continued into October. On 14 September she
replied to his letter of the previous day:

I could refute every charge you
allege against me in your letter; but I
revere a man, either in deep love or in
deep grief: and as it is impossible to
convince, I would at least say nothing
to irritate him.

Yet surely thus much I may venture
to add. As the short and very slight
acquaintance I had with Mrs. Godwin, and
into which I was reluctantly impelled by
you, has been productive of petty
suspicions and revilings (from which my
character has been till now preserved),
surely I cannot sufficiently applaud my
own penetration in apprehending, and my
own firmness in resisting, a longer and
more familiar acquaintance.[54]

By the end of October she finally dismissed him,
writing on 26 October:

With the most sincere sympathy in
all you have suffered - with the most
perfect forgiveness of all you have said
to me, there must nevertheless be an end
to our acquaintance _for ever_. I respect
your prejudices, but I also respect _my_
own.[55]

For the time being, at any rate, Godwin had
to accept Elizabeth's act of estrangement. He was
writing his memoirs of Mary, initially to be
entitled, Memoirs of the Author of the Rights of
Woman; it was written with such passion and candor
that it was received by some as 'discreditable to
them both,' since it shows Mary Godwin to have been
a 'woman without religion, without delicacy,
without shame.' Robert Southey was to allege that
it showed a 'want of feeling in stripping his dead

wife naked.'[56]   But it is in fact a work of great
courage, great love and sincerity, greatly to
Godwin's credit.

In 1798 his widower's status began to cause
him trouble. The nurse, Louisa Jane, hired to look
after Mary's two little girls and procured by his
sister Harriet for him, showed signs that she
expected him to marry her and so (it would seem)
hastened his own proposals of marriage in the
summer of 1798 to a schoolmistress in Bath, Mrs.
Harriet Lee, who was a poetess and dramatist. She
rejected him because he was a non-believer. In
1799, the year he published his novel, St. Leon, he
made a further attempt at reconciliation with
Elizabeth, sending her a copy of the novel. She
replied in terms which, in spite of surface
friendliness, made it clear that further intimacy
between them was at an end. Godwin had written on
28 November 1799:

> I determined to request your
> acceptance of a copy of my novel, and to
> ask you seriously whether you did not
> think two years' banishment, expiation
> sufficient for a reproach which you,
> slowly and reluctantly on my part, wrung
> from me, at a period the most painful
> and agonizing in human life. I allow
> you ten days from the date of this ...
> that you feel an invincible repugnance,
> if you can be so severe, to the renewal
> of our acquaintance. If I do not hear
> from you by that time, I shall then
> venture to come to your habitation.[57]

Elizabeth's reply was dated 4 December:

> ... you judged perfectly right that
> I could not have expressed any
> resentment against you, for I have long
> ago felt none. I also assure you that
> it will always give me great pleasure to
> meet you in company with others, but to
> receive satisfaction in your society as
> a familiar visitor at my own house I
> never can.
>
> Impressions made on me are
> lasting. Your conversation and manners

were once agreeable to me, and will ever be so. But while I retain the memory of all your good qualities, I trust you will allow me not to forget your bad ones; but warily to guard against those painful and humiliating effects, which the event of my singular circumstances might once again produce. Your admirer and friend. E. Inchbald.[58]

Three weeks later she sent him a critique of St. Leon.

It was Mary Wollstonecraft's daughter, Mary Godwin, later to become the wife of Shelley, who was to leave us one of the near-contemporary descriptions of Elizabeth, a description no doubt colored by her father's view of the woman the loss of whose friendship he deplored. She wrote:

Nothing can be more singular and interesting than the picture of her life as given in her biography. Living in mean lodgings, dressed with an economy allied to penury, without connections, and alone, her beauty, her talents, and the charm of her manners gave her entrance into a delightful circle of society. Apt to fall in love, and desirous to marry, she continued single, because the men who loved and admired her were too worldly to take an actress and a poor author, however lovely and charming, for a wife. Her life was thus spent in an interchange of hardship and amusement, privation and luxury. Her character partook of the same contrast: fond of pleasure, she was prudent in her conduct; penurious in her personal expenditures, she was generous to others. Vain of her beauty, we are told that the gown she wore was not worth a shilling, it was so coarse and shabby. Very susceptible to the softer feelings, she could yet guard herself against passion, and although she might have been called a flirt, her character was unimpeached. I have heard that a rival beauty of her day pettishly complained that when Mrs. Inchbald came into a room, and sat in a chair in the middle of it as was her wont, every man gathered round it, and it was vain for any other woman to attempt to gain attention. Godwin could not fail to admire her; she became and continued to be a favorite. Her talents, her beauty, her manners were all delightful to him. He used to describe her as a piquante mixture between a lady and a milkmaid, and added that Sheridan declared she was the only authoress whose society pleased him.[59]

It can be compared with that left by Fanny (Frances Ann) Kemble, John Philip Kemble's niece:

She was very beautiful, and gifted with original genius, as her plays and farces and novels (above all, the "Simple Story") testify; she was not an actress of any special merit, but of respectable mediocrity. She stuttered habitually, but her delivery was never impeded by this defect on the stage; ... Mrs. Inchbald was a person of a very remarkable character, lovely, poor, with unusual mental powers and of irreproachable conduct .... Mrs. Inchbald had a singular uprightness and unworldliness, and a childlike directness and simplicity of manner, which, combined with her personal loveliness and halting, broken utterance, gave to her conversation, which was both humorous and witty, a most peculiar and comical charm.[60]

Nature and Art (1796)

Nature and Art is a short novel of only some 50,000 words. According to Boaden, it was completed early in 1794 and therefore written during the height of the so-called Jacobin period in England, and during the key period in Elizabeth's involvement with Holcroft and especially with Godwin. Godwin's own first venture into fiction, Caleb Williams, had appeared two years before during the very period of the Treason Trials (1793-94) and Holcroft's imprisonment, incidents which undoubtedly delayed publication of

Elizabeth's comparatively innocuous novel – innocuous, that is, from any strictly political standpoint. With its profound misgivings over judicial procedures and practices in the English courts of law, Godwin's novel had greatly excited her, and there was as yet no Mary Wollstonecraft in London to distract Godwin's attention from her.

Nature and Art is therefore Elizabeth's contribution to the Jacobin novel,[61] and it is a socio-political fable rather than a realistic or domestic novel in the manner of A Simple Story. Read now, it has a curiously Shavian touch to it, unashamedly 'didactic' in an amusing way, gilding the moral with wit, and the action with a certain naturalistic melodrama, the tragedy of Agnes. It was not, however, anything like as popular as A Simple Story. As Hazlitt was to put it in On the English Novelists:

> Mrs. Inchbald's Nature and Art would scarcely have had the same popularity [as Mrs. Radcliffe's work] but that it fell in (as to its two main characters) with the prevailing prejudice of the moment, that judges and bishops were not invariably pure abstractions of justice and piety.[62]

The story begins with two teenage brothers, William and Henry Norwynne, who become orphans on the death of their father, and who walk to London in search of employment. After a fruitless period in the capital, it is only Henry's ability to play the violin with some distinction (like Rousseau and Holcroft) which secured him popularity and patronage, while William, peevish at his ill-fortune but anxious for a classical education, went to 'one of these seats of learning' (that is, either Oxford or Cambridge), where he was able to study to become a clergyman in the Anglican church through the good fortune of his brother in London, who secures him the patronage of a noble. William's character, however, hardens with learning and piety; he becomes contemptuous of the brother who had done everything to help him, and the brothers are finally estranged when Henry marries a 'public singer.' William, given a comfortable benefice by his noble patron, marries Lady Clementina, a socialite snob, daughter of a Scottish aristocrat. Both brothers have sons, but when Henry's wife dies in childbirth, he departs with his infant child (young Henry) for Africa. Meanwhile, William prospers in the Church, becomes a stern-faced Dean, rearing his child (young William) in the conventional manner, thus ensuring his thorough mis-education.

This is by way of prologue. The main part of the novel begins with the unexpected arrival of young Henry by himself from Africa; he has a letter written by his father, languishing in captivity by savages, asking the Dean in effect to adopt his 12-year-old son and rear him in England. The Dean receives his nephew kindly enough, but it is soon apparent that the child has been brought up à la Rousseau (that is, he has received from his father a 'natural' education), and that therefore his 'natural' intelligence constantly brings into question the experience of living in a strictly orthodox, upperclass, 18th century Christian household.[63] Young Henry's innate honesty of mind constantly distresses and disconcerts the Dean, but they strive for his soul's sake to convert him to a more conventional outlook and hypocrisy of speech.

The two boys become young men, and the contrast between them is next revealed in their attitude to women. Young William seduces Agnes,[64] the daughter of a cottager, and deserts her when she is pregnant, in spite of the pitiful love letter she manages to compose, appealing to him to help her. The Dean proposes a marriage of social convenience to a Miss Sedgeley, which young William accepts, turning aside from the constant pleas of the deserted Agnes. Young Henry, on the other hand, has established a happy, progressive relationship with Rebecca, the somewhat homely daughter of a curate of the parish, a well-read, thoughtful girl. Henry rescues an abandoned baby, and Rebecca, generous and kindly, at once accepts it in her care, even though it leads to her being accused by her family of being its mother, and with Henry being regarded as the father. In consequence, Henry is turned out of the Dean's house on the very eve of William's wedding. He leaves for Africa to search for his long-lost father.

Meanwhile, Agnes, who is contemplating

suicide, has admitted to Henry that the baby is hers, and offers to clear Rebecca's name; circumstances drive her to reveal the identity of the child's father to the Dean himself. This only leads to his determination to have the matter 'hushed up' and that the child (now Agnes's only comfort) be immediately taken from her and put in care. As the Dean is a magistrate as well as a cleric, he has the power to effect this. Agnes has no employment and in despair departs for London, where she is continuously unfortunate and ends up a prostitute and a thief.

The years have passed. The elder William lives in affluence and has become a Bishop. Nevertheless, he is not happy, and his vain and stupid wife remains a constant affliction to him. He is also conscience-stricken that he had ill-used his kindly brother. The elder Henry, an exile in Africa for 23 years, is finally reunited with his beloved son, who has been searching for him for two years. Back in England, young William has become a judge, and passes sentence of death on Agnes, who has been brought before his court, and whom he does not recognize. Only after she has been executed does he come to realize who she was, and that her 16-year-old son is also his. But it is too late; he has pined away, dying two days after his mother's execution.

A year later, the two Henrys, the elder and the younger, return to England, destitute. They find that the Bishop has died, and that William has divorced his wife for adultery. Rebecca, however, has remained faithful to young Henry, and they become happily married and, living along with the elder Henry, self-sufficient by their own simple industry, and dependent economically on no one.

In a sense, <u>Nature and Art</u> takes up where <u>A Simple Story</u> leaves off, with insistence on a rightful attitude to education. It is definitely influenced by Rousseau, and especially by his <u>Emile</u>.[65] Young Henry is the son of a liberal father and a child of <u>nature</u>, having been reared by his father as a man of 'sense and sensibility' among 'savages' (whether 'noble' or otherwise is not indicated, though they certainly treat the elder Henry very badly when he is no longer able to play his violin for them); young William, on the other hand, is conceived as the product of 'art,' son of a 'corrupted' father and the typical product of the prejudices and artifices of 'civilized' convention. However, William McKee, writing some fifty years ago in his study of Elizabeth as novelist, considers that she became so concerned about the female protagonist, Agnes, and her terrible fate at the hands of an unjust society (she is treated as badly as Caleb Williams in Godwin's novel), that she turns increasingly aside from what should have been her central, Jacobin-influenced theme, the effects of two contrasting systems of education on the two young cousins. He considers the space devoted to the network of characters (the 'villains,' the Dean and his son, and the 'heroes,' the expatriate musician and his son, and the two 'heroines,' the weak, loving girl, Agnes, and the strong, loving girl, Rebecca) thrown out of true by the overstressed development of Agnes at the expense of Rebecca and young William and his father at the expense (finally) of young Henry and his father, as if Elizabeth had lost interest in the very man who should have been the central core of the book throughout - young Henry. Indeed, throughout the novel, the Dean (the elder William) tends to dominate the male cast as by far the strongest-drawn character. Once again, McKee suggests the dramatist in Elizabeth takes over from the didact and concentrates on the villain William and his victim Agnes for the story's sake, once young Henry's virtues have become fully established. He holds her to be an amateur as far as the structure of her novels and the deployment of her characters are concerned.

Writing far more recently, Gary Kelly considers that Nature and Art may well be the final outcome of the script, Satire upon our Times, which Boaden claims was abandoned on advice, in particular, of George Hardinge, who, as one of the Queen's attorneys-general, either personally disapproved of it or was in a position to warn her against publication in 1794, since he would know that the Treason Trials were to be held late in the year. He also recognized that the character of Lord Rinforth the Lord of the Bedchamber, was intended to represent the King himself, George III. He also claims that Dean William Norwynne was a satirical portrait of Bishop Horsley, also the model for Dr. Block in Robert Bage's Hermsprong and the gourmand Bishop in Holcroft's Hugh Trevor, since he wins his promotion to Bishop by writing pro-government pamphlets, just as Horsley in 1794 was presented with the see of Rochester for his pro-government, anti-revolutionary sermons and his heartless condemnation of the poor.

However derivative or disguised these parallels, the power of Nature and Art lies in its satiric exposure of inequity, hypocrisy and injustice in British society, promulgated largely in the name of Christianity. The quality of its satire gives the book its immediacy and freshness for the modern reader and to a considerable extent overcomes its weakness of structure, which shows little, if any, improvement on that of A Simple Story. There are constant time lapses somewhat awkwardly indicated by bald statements of fact. The chapters are all very brief. William and Henry the elder are teenagers in Chapter I, adults by Chapter IV, married and fathers by Chapter VI. After a sudden lapse of some twelve years, young Henry takes up residence in the Dean's household in Chapter X, and by Chapter XX he and his cousin are old enough to have their love affairs with Rebecca and Agnes, with sad consequences for both women. By Chapter XXXVI Agnes's child is well-grown and with her in London, and in Chapters XL and XLI she is condemned and executed. In Chapter XLIII young Henry returns to London after his two-year search for his father, and this short novel ends with Henry the elder and the younger, together with Rebecca, happily settled in their humble dwelling by the sea. The time-span of this account must be little less than half a century, covered in no less than 47 chapters averaging little more than one thousand words each.

Also out of balance, as already suggested, is the fact that the protagonists become the Dean and his son rather than the nominal 'heroes,' the elder and the younger Henry. The elder Henry in effect disappears entirely through the greater part of the story. Neither Rebecca nor even Agnes command much space in the action. This seems due to the fact that Elizabeth's principal interest in the story is human exposure of 'things as they are,' which she achieves with considerable satiric wit, while her promotion of Rousseauism is left increasingly to

implication as the novel proceeds - Henry the
younger's undoubted goodness of heart and soundness
of values being taken for granted once his
character has become established. No detailed
account is given of his childhood education in
Africa - Nature and Art is no Emile in English
clothing. However, young William's education is
briefly touched upon and contrasted with that of
Henry, as described in his father's letter to the
Dean, his brother.

Young William passed his time, from
morning till night, with persons who
taught him to walk, to ride, to talk, to
think like a man - a foolish man,
instead of a wise child, as nature
designed him to be.

This unfortunate youth was never
permitted to have one conception of his
own - all were taught him - he was never
once asked, 'What he thought;' but men
were paid to tell 'how to think.' He
was taught to revere such and such
persons, however unworthy of his
reverence; to believe such and such
things, however unworthy of his credit;
and to act so and so, on such and such
occasions, however unworthy of his
feelings.

Such were the lessons of the tutors
assigned him by his father - those
masters whom his mother gave him did him
less mischief; for though they distorted
his limbs and made his manners
effeminate, they did not interfere
beyond the body.

Mr. Norwynne (the family name of
his father, and though but a school-boy,
he was called Mister) could talk on
history, on politics, and on religion;
surprisingly to all who never listened
to a parrot or magpie - for he merely
repeated what had been told to him
without one reflection upon the sense or
probability of his report. He had been
praised for his memory; and to continue
that praise, he was so anxious to retain

114

every sentence he had heard, or he had read, that the poor creature had no time for one native idea, but could only re-deliver his tutors' lessons to his father, and his father's to his tutors. But, whatever he said or did, was the admiration of all who came to the house of the dean, and who knew he was an only child. Indeed, considering the labour that was taken to spoil him, he was rather a commendable youth; for, with the pedantic folly of his teachers, the blind affection of his father and mother, the obsequiousness of the servants, and flattery of the visitors, it was some credit to him that he was not an idiot, or a brute - though when he imitated the manners of a man, he had something of the latter in his appearance; for he would grin and bow to a lady, catch her fan in haste when it fell, and hand her to her coach, as thoroughly void of all the sentiment which gives grace to such tricks, as a monkey 66

Not having any books here, I have only been able to teach my child by talking to him, and in all my conversations with him I have never taken much pains to instruct him in the manners of my own country; thinking, that if ever he went over, he would learn them soon enough; and if he never did go over, that it would be as well he knew nothing about them.

I have kept him also from the knowledge of everything which I have thought pernicious in the conduct of the savages, except that I have now and then pointed out a few of their faults, in order to give him a true conception and a proper horror of them. At the same time I have taught him to love, and to do good to his neighbour, whoever that neighbour may be, and whatever may be his failings. Falsehood of every kind I included in this precept as forbidden, for no one can love his neighbour and deceive him.

> I have instructed him too, to hold
> in contempt all frivolous vanity, and
> all those indulgences which he was never
> likely to obtain. He has learnt all
> that I have undertaken to teach him, but
> I am afraid you will yet think he has
> learned too little.[67]

Rebecca, like Elizabeth herself, is (as an
impoverished clergyman's daughter) an autodidact,
though with the advantage at least of free access
to a well-stocked library:

> Rebecca was the youngest, and by
> far the least handsome daughter of four,
> to whom the Reverend Mr. Rymer, a
> widower, was father. The other sisters
> were accounted beauties; and she, from
> her comparative want of personal charms,
> having been less beloved by her parents,
> and less caressed by those who visited
> them, than the rest, had for some time
> past sought other resources of happiness
> than the affection, praise, and
> indulgence of her fellow-creatures. The
> parsonage house in which this family
> lived was the forlorn remains of an
> ancient abbey: it had in later times
> been the habitation of a rich and
> learned rector, by whom, at his decease,
> a library was bequeathed for the use of
> every succeeding resident. Rebecca,
> left alone in this huge ruinous abode,
> while her sisters were paying stated
> visits in search of admiration, passed
> her solitary hours in reading. She not
> merely read - she thought: the choicest
> English books from this excellent
> library taught her to think; and
> reflection fashioned her mind to bear
> the slights, the mortifications of
> neglect, with a patient dejection,
> rather than with an indignant or a
> peevish spirit.

> This resignation to injury and
> contumely gave to her perfect symmetry
> of person, a timid eye, a retiring

manner, and spread upon her face a
placid sweetness, a pale serenity
indicating sense, which no wise
connoisseur in female charms would have
exchanged for all the sparkling eyes and
florid tints of her vain and vulgar
sisters.[68]

It is the character of the Dean, his worldly
wife and young William in adult life that Elizabeth
gives her fullest attention. She exposes the
future Dean's harsh condescension to his brother,
the accomplished musician, to whose skill as a
violinist he owes his education:

Henry's renown in his profession
daily increased; and, with his fame, his
friends. Possessing the virtues of
humility and charity far above William,
who was the professed teacher of those
virtues, his reverend brother's
disrespect for his vocation never once
made him relax for a moment his anxiety
to gain his advancement in the Church.
In the course of a few years, and in
consequence of many fortuitous
circumstances, he had the gratification
of procuring for him the appointment to
a deanery, and thus at once placed
between them an insurmountable barrier
to all friendship, that was not the
effect of condescension on the part of
the Dean.[69]

Elizabeth condemns the nature of the Dean's wife,
Lady Clementina, and the hypocrisy of their
marriage:

If she complained she was ill, it
was with the certainty that her languor
would be admired; if she boasted she was
well, it was that the spectator might
admire her glowing health; if she
laughed, it was because she thought it
made her look pretty; if she cried, it
was because she thought it made her look
prettier still. If she scolded her
servants, it was from vanity, to show
her knowledge superior to theirs; and
she was kind to them from the same

117

motive, that her benevolence might
excite their admiration. Forward and
impertinent in the company of her
equals, from the vanity of supposing
herself above them, she was bashful even
to shamefacedness in the presence of her
superiors, because her vanity told her
she engrossed all their observation.
Through vanity she had no memory; for
she constantly forgot everything she
heard others say, from the minute
attention which she paid to everything
she said herself.[70]

Also:

If the Dean had loved his wife but
moderately, seeing all her faults
clearly as he did, he must frequently
have quarrelled with her: if he had
loved her with tenderness, he must have
treated her with a degree of violence in
the hope of amending her failings. But
having neither personal nor mental
affection towards her sufficiently
interesting to give himself the trouble
to contradict her will in anything, he
passed for one of the best husbands in
the world. Lady Clementina went out
when she liked, stayed at home when she
liked, dressed as she liked, and talked
as she liked without a word of
disapprobation from her husband, and all
- because he cared nothing about her
.... The dean's wife being a fine lady -
while her husband and his friend pored
over books or their own manuscripts at
home, she ran from house to house, from
public amusement to public amusement;
but much less for the pleasure of seeing
than for that of being seen. Nor was it
material to her enjoyment whether she
were observed, or welcomed, where she
went, as she never entertained the
smallest doubt of either; but rested
assured that her presence roused
curiosity and dispensed gladness all
around.[71]

Satire extends to the social hypocrisies of

118

the time to which the Dean conforms:

> Let the reader understand, that the
> dean, fondly attached to every ornament
> of his dignified function, was never
> seen (unless caught in bed) without an
> enormous wig! With this young Henry was
> enormously struck; having never seen so
> unbecoming a decoration, either in the
> savage island from whence he came, or on
> board the vessel in which he sailed.

> 'Do you imagine,' cried his uncle,
> laying his hand gently on the reverend
> habiliment, 'that this grows?'

> 'What is on my head grows,' said
> young Henry, 'and so does that which is
> upon my father's.'

> 'But now you are come to Europe,
> Henry, you will see many persons with
> such things as these, which they put on
> and take off.'

> 'Why do you wear such things?'

> 'As a distinction between us and
> inferior people: they are worn to give
> an importance to the wearer.'

> 'That's just as the savages do;
> they hang brass nails, wire, buttons,
> and entrails of beasts all over them, to
> give them importance.[72]

The Dean's most immediate patron is a Bishop,
to whom he pays adulatory attention, including
permitting the Bishop's name to be attached to
certain of the reactionary writings he composes in
support of maintaining 'things as they are.' This
the innocent and Rousseauesque Henry finds hard to
understand:

> Henry had frequently, in his
> conversation, betrayed the total want of
> all knowledge in respect to religion or
> futurity, and the dean for this reason
> delayed taking him to church, till he
> had previously given him instructions

119

<u>wherefore</u> he went.

A leisure morning arrived, on which he took his nephew to his study, and implanted in his youthful mind the first unconfused idea of the Creator of the universe!

The dean was eloquent. Henry was all attention; his understanding, expanded by time to the conception of a God - and not warped by custom from the sensations which a just notion of that God inspires - dwelt with delight and wonder on the information given him - lessons which, instilled into the head of a senseless infant, too often produce, throughout his remaining life, an impious indifference to the truths revealed.

Yet, with all that astonished, that respectful sensibility which Henry showed on this great occasion, he still expressed his opinion, and put questions to the dean, with his usual simplicity, till he felt himself convinced.

'What!' cried he - after being informed of the attributes inseparable from the Supreme Being, and having received the injunction to offer prayers to Him night and morning - 'What! am I permitted to speak to Power Divine?'

'At all times,' replied the dean.

'How! whenever I like?'

'Whenever you like,' returned the Dean.

'I durst not,' cried Henry, 'make so free with the bishop, nor dare any of his attendants.'

'The bishop,' said the dean, 'is the servant of God, and therefore must be treated with respect.[73]

Most painful of all to Elizabeth seems to be the Dean's attitude to the poor, which offends her humanity most deeply, both as Christian and Rousseauist. She returns to this subject again and again:

'There are in society,' continued the dean, 'rich and poor; the poor are born to serve the rich.'

'And what are the rich born for?'

'To be served by the poor.'

'But suppose the poor would not serve them?'

'Then they must starve.'

'And so poor people are permitted to live only upon condition that they wait upon the rich?'

'Is that a hard condition; or if it were, they will be rewarded in a better world than this?'

'Is there a better world than this?'

'Is it possible you do not know there is?'

'I heard my father once say something about a world to come, but he stopped short and said I was too young to understand what he meant.'

'The world to come,' returned the dean, 'is where we shall go after death; and there no distinction will be made between rich and poor - all persons there will be equal.'

'Aye, now I see what makes it a better world than this. But cannot this world try to be as good as that?'

'In respect to placing all persons on a level, it is utterly impossible. God has ordained it otherwise.'

121

'How! has God ordained a distinction to be made, and will not make any Himself?'[74]

The Dean, indeed, is the author of a pamphlet praising Britain as the best of all possible places in which to live:

> This pamphlet glowed with the dean's love for his country; and such a country as he described, it was impossible <u>not</u> to love. 'Salubrious air, fertile fields, wood, water, corn, grass, sheep, oxen, fish, fowl, fruit, and vegetables,' were dispersed with the most prodigal hand; 'valiant men, virtuous women; statesmen wise and just; tradesmen abounding in merchandise and money; husbandmen possessing peace, ease, plenty; and all ranks liberty.' This brilliant description, while the dean read the work to his family, so charmed poor Henry, that he repeatedly cried out,

> 'I am glad I came to this country.'

> But it so happened that a few days after, Lady Clementina, in order to render the delicacy of her taste admired, could eat of no one dish upon the table, but found fault with them all. The dean at length said to her,

> 'Indeed, you are too nice; reflect upon the hundreds of poor creatures who have not a morsel or a drop of anything to subsist upon, except bread and water; and even of the first a scanty allowance, but for which they are obliged to toil six days in the week, from sun to sun.'

> 'Pray, uncle,' cried Henry, 'in what country do these poor people live?'

> 'In this country,' replied the dean.

> Henry rose from his chair, ran to the chimney-piece, took up his uncle's

122

pamphlet, and said, 'I don't remember your mentioning them here.'

'Perhaps I have not,' answered the dean, coolly.

Still Henry turned over each leaf of the book, but he could meet only with luxurious details of 'the fruits of the earth, the beasts of the field, the birds of the air, and the fishes of the sea.'

'Why, here is provision enough for all the people,' said Henry; 'why should they want? why do not they go and take some of these things?'

'They must not,' said the dean, 'unless they were their own.'

'What, uncle! does no part of the earth, nor anything which the earth produces, belong to the poor?'

'Certainly not.'

'Why did not you say so, then, in your pamphlet?'

'Because it is what everybody knows.'

'Oh, then, what you have said in your pamphlet is only what - nobody knows.'

There appeared to the dean, in the delivery of this sentence, a satirical acrimony, which his irritability as an author could but ill forgive.[75]

The Dean also takes advantage of his superior social position to force religion down the throats of the poor:

... rigid attention to the religion and morals of people in poverty, and total neglect of their bodily wants, was the Dean's practice. He forced them to

123

attend church every Sabbath; but whether they had a dinner on their return was too gross and temporal an enquiry for his spiritual fervour. Good of the soul was all he aimed at; and this pious undertaking, besides his diligence as a pastor, required all his exertion as a magistrate - for to be very poor and very honest, very oppressed and yet very thankful, is a degree of sainted excellence not often to be attained, without the aid of zealous men to frighten into virtue.[76]

Once Agnes is revealed to the Dean as the mother of an illegitimate child she has left abandoned, the full weight of his inhumanity falls upon her, since he is the magistrate as well as the dignitary of the church. When she finally gathers courage to reveal to the Dean that his own son (just married) is the father of her child, he insists that the matter be kept strictly secret, and refuses to give the betrayed woman any help in her predicament.

So _Nature and Art_, in spite of the implications of its unusual title, leans increasingly in the direction of drama, and even melodrama, because its author's bent is that of the entertainer rather than the teacher. Once she had made her main standpoint clear in contrasting the two brothers and their respective sons, the story as such takes over and the moral is left to take care of itself. In her second novel Elizabeth proves herself still to be the dramatist at heart, set on establishing dramatic situations and confrontations that lie within the framework of her novel.

Thomas Holcroft
Portrait (1805) published in
The British Theatre

126

IV

CRITIC AND HISTORIAN OF
THE BRITISH DRAMA

By the turn of the century Elizabeth Inchbald
had become one of the most respected of writers in
the mainstream of literary output in England. It
was a transitional period in English writing, with
the powerful influence of the French revolution of
the 1790s only too evident, like a sting in the
tail. In an age that seemed to enjoy both writing
and reading literary and dramatic criticism on a
higher level than the immediate and ephemeral
reports in the press, Elizabeth could also hold her
own as a critical essayist. Her position was so
well established by the early 19th century for her
to be invited to become a regular contributor to
the newly-established Quarterly Review, though she
chose not to do so, since by this time, when she
was in her mid-fifties, her energies had become
limited.

It was therefore no surprise when in 1806 she
was invited to write critical and biographical
introductions to a generous selection of
representative plays from Shakespeare's time to the
close of the 18th century which were regarded by
the publisher as being of sufficient note to be
anthologized in a series which appeared at first
periodically and was later finally assembled in
1808 in 25 volumes, each including five plays - 125
in all. It would seem that these plays were not
selected by Elizabeth in the first place, but by
the publisher, and that the choice, looked at with
hindsight almost two centuries later, might appear
somewhat arbitrary. No doubt at the time the
choice was based on the popularity the pieces had
enjoyed in the late 18th-century theatre (often
through association with some star performance
rather than as a result of pure dramatic merit), or
on the achievement of a satisfactory sale at the
time of their initial publication. In the case of
Shakespeare, however, 24 of his plays were
included, filling the first five volumes in the
series, with Ben Jonson's Every Man in his Humour

(the only one of his plays represented) completing
the fifth volume. Marked omissions are Marlowe,
Webster and Ford, while the Restoration dramatists
are comparatively thinly represented in heavily
bowdlerized versions. On the other hand, Cibber
and Rowe have four plays each, Cumberland five, and
Colman the Younger no less than eight. Elizabeth
herself has five plays included - one a translation
from Kotzebue - filling Volume XX.

Elizabeth explains the terms of her
commission in an open letter dated March 1808 and
addressed to George Colman the Younger, who had
complained about certain points in her critical
introduction to his father's plays and his own:

> I accepted an overture, to write
> from two to four pages, in the manner of
> preface, to be introduced before a
> certain number of plays, for the
> perusal, or information, of such persons
> as have not access to any diffuse
> compositions, either in biography or
> criticism, but who are yet very liberal
> contributors to the treasury of a
> theatre .... One of the points of my
> agreement was, that I should have no
> control over the time or the order in
> which these prefaces were to be printed
> or published, but that I should merely
> produce them as they were called for,
> and resign all other interference to the
> proprietor or editor of the work ....
> Nor did the time or space allotted me,
> for both observations and biography (for
> biography of the deceased was part of my
> duty, and not introduced at my
> discretion), admit of any farther than
> an abridgement, or slight sketch, of
> each.[1]

What in fact Elizabeth offers her readers
amounts in all to some 20,000 or more words, giving
basic biographical accounts of the dramatists and
some background to their plays, together with often
acute and pointed criticism from the point of view
of a woman of the theatre. She is very well aware
of the difference between scripts written for
professional production - plays which
flesh-and-blood players must perform successfully to

flesh-and-blood audiences who have given of their time and money to patronize the living theatre - and plays that are literary exercises, written, as she puts it, for the 'closet,' not the stage. She is full of praise for memorable performances by star players in theatrically effective parts. While Shakespeare remains the dominating figure among British dramatists (with his 24 works reproduced as against everyone else being represented by anything between one to eight plays), Dr. Johnson figures as the most respected critic, whom she frequently cites. But she is never afraid to criticize on her own account, even the plays of contemporary dramatists she knows personally. George Colman the Younger was indeed, as we have seen, stung to reply to her strictures, and his open letter of reproach and her equally open reply appear in the 21st volume. It should be remembered that women commentators or critics (as distinct from creative writers) were virtually unknown in the early 19th century; writing as late as 1833, Boaden in the <u>Memoirs</u> says, 'There is something unfeminine ... in a lady's placing herself in the seat of judgment.' Her comments, he says, made her unpopular with her contemporaries, and 'added but little to her fortune and nothing whatever to her fame.' Her initial retaining fee amounted to only 60 guineas, and she even appears to have tried to get released from her contract. Boaden claims that the pieces were written 'with slender preparation.'[2]

Elizabeth's values are unmistakably those of the late 18th century. As Prof. Allardyce Nicoll, for example, points out in the volume of his <u>History of the English Drama</u> devoted to the later 18th century, audiences had changed somewhat from the rough and rowdy houses of an earlier age; they were 'quieter and less uproarious' than the patrons of the Restoration period, who had clamoured in response to plays like unruly adolescents, even invading the stage itself. Audiences in Elizabeth's time preferred 'highly decorous comic operas,' 'moral melodramas' and 'decorous sentimental comedies' which emphasized 'poetic justice.' They liked productions which involved spectacular settings that displayed the artistry of the stage designer and scene painter. They were inspired by 'sensibility,' the catchword of the time; audiences were expected to demonstrate openly

that they were men and women of feeling combined
with the niceties of prudery, so that commentators
such as Elizabeth could use in describing such
emotional responses the word 'genteel.'[3]

Not that members of these same audiences
could not become rowdy with disapproval at times
and dispute from the auditorium with actors on the
stage. Holcroft, writing in the 1780s, describes
the drunks who could get into the theatre and cause
disturbances ('the nightly intrusion of unhappy and
improper persons'), while a Prologue to a play by
Mrs. Cowley in the 1790s refers to the pressure of
bodies in the pit:

> Ah! ah! you're here, and comfortably
> tight?
> Well squeez'd and press'd, I see - from
> left to right.

Audiences could only too easily grow inattentive
and chatter during the performance. Elizabeth,
with the memories of an actress as well as of a
dramatist, was well aware that she and her fellow
players depended on the dramatists not only to give
them playable plays which could hold the attention
of at any rate the bulk of the audience, but work
which would not offend the growing body of genteel,
middle-class people who came to the theatre as
families and did not want to have their ears (or
those of their adolescent daughters) offended by
the obscene and scurrilous dialogue that had once
delighted the city rakes and their doxies in
earlier times.

Elizabeth herself stood in the van of these
reforms, which unhappily went hand in hand with the
decline of creative vitality in dramatic writing.
Only in comedy, particularly the comedy of manners,
did the dramatists of the late 18th century hold
their own, among them Elizabeth. Again and again
she emphasizes the importance of playwrights
supplying plays suitable for polite audiences: of
Romeo and Juliet she says, 'it seldom attracts an
elegant audience.' 'The company,' she adds, 'will
not come to a tragedy, unless to weep in torrents -
and Romeo and Juliet will not draw even a copious
shower of tears.' Southerne's Isabella (in which
Sarah Siddons failed in her first, youthful debut
for Garrick in London), was more to their taste; it

was a tragedy that 'effectually wrung the hearts of those who possess nice sensibility.' She is happy that in Mrs. Cowley's The Belle's Stratagem, 'the persons of importance ... are all elegant, or, at least, well bred.' She praises Steele's The Conscious Lovers because it is 'elegantly written, highly refined,' and notes that Garrick adapted Wycherley's The Country Wife as The Country Girl by 'expunging those parts ... which an improved taste delicately rejects.' In matters of taste, anything 'coarse,' including even dialogue in dialect - which was sometimes introduced by some dramatists, such as Holcroft or Colman the Younger for the benefit of 'low' comedians - was to be rejected. She pleads with Colman in her preface to his John Bull to 'leave the distortion of language to men who cannot embellish it like yourself,' merely to provide dialogue suitable for low comedy. Dialect, she writes, belongs to 'common life,' and is but 'language ... deformed,' which on the stage produces 'uncouth sounds' that 'pervade ... the ear.' She castigates Cibber for She Wou'd and She Wou'd Not - 'This comedy has neither wit nor sentiment - it has, instead, swearing, lying, and imposture,' though she praises it afterwards for its 'dexterous' plot and 'bold characters.' And in the preface to her friend, Thomas Holcroft's play, The Road to Ruin, she says:

> Coarse manners, like old age, should always be counterfeit on the stage: when either of these is inherent in the actor himself, as well as in the character he represents, the sensitive part of the audience are more afflicted than entertained.

Similarly, she stresses the need for the theatre to establish and sustain its moral standards. This puts her in something of a dilemma when faced with the coarser elements in Shakespeare's plays, and with the wits of the Restoration whose plays still survived on the later 18th century stage, though severely pruned and altered. She is unsparing in her condemnation of the immorality of these plays:

> Of Farquhar's The Beaux' Stratagem: The well drawn characters, happy incidents, and excellent dialogue,

in <u>The Beaux' Strategem</u>, are but poor atonement for that unrestrained contempt of principle which pervades every scene. Plays of this kind are far more mischievous than those, which preserve less appearance of delicacy. Every auditor and reader shrinks from those crimes, which are recommended in unseemly language, and from libertinism united with coarse manners; but in adorning vice with wit, and audacious rakes with the vivacity and elegance of men of fashion, youth, at least, will be decoyed into the snare of admiration.

Of Mrs. Centlivre's <u>A Bold Stroke for a Wife</u>: The authoress of this comedy should have laid down her pen, and taken, in exchange, the meanest implement of labour, rather than have imitated the licentious example given her by the renowned poets of those days .... Nor can her offence be treated with excessive rigour in reference to the present time by those who consider that this very play of <u>A Bold Stroke for a Wife</u> is now frequently performed to an elegant, yet applauding audience.

Of Gay's <u>The Beggar's Opera</u> she writes that, 'it has the fatal tendency to make vice alluring.'

On a more positive note, what Elizabeth looked for in all plays, but especially in those of her contemporaries, was 'credibility' and a closeness to 'Nature.' She applied this to Shakespeare, objecting on this account to both <u>Romeo and Juliet</u> and <u>Cymbeline</u>; of the latter she says:

the impossibility, that half the events in this play could ever occur, cannot be the sole cause of its weak effect. Shakespeare's scenes are frequently such, as could not take place in real life; and yet the sensations which they excite are so forcible, that improbability is overpowered by the author's art, and his auditors are made to feel, though they cannot believe. No

such magic presides over the play of
Cymbeline as to transform reason into
imagination.

Credibility remains a constant theme in Elizabeth's
assessment of more contemporary drama; she praises
the authenticity of George Lillo's realistic drama,
Fatal Curiosity, in spite of the violence in it
against which she warns both readers and spectators:

> From the first scene of this
> tragedy to the last, all is interesting,
> all is natural - occurrences, as in real
> life, give rise to passions; passion
> inspires new thoughts, elevates each
> sentiment, embellishes the language, and
> renders every page of the production
> either sweetly pathetic, or horribly
> sublime .... Mr. Colman was a warm
> admirer of Lillo's works, and of this
> play in particular. He caused it to be
> rehearsed with infinite care; and, from
> the reception of the first two acts, and
> part of the third, he had the hope that
> it would become extremely popular - but,
> on the performance of a scene which
> followed soon after, a certain horror
> seized the audience, and was manifested
> by a kind of stifled scream. After
> having shuddered at this tragedy, even
> as a fiction, it is dreadful to be told,
> - that the most horrid event which here
> takes place, is merely the
> representation of a fact which occurred
> at a village on the western coast of
> England.4

She praises the naturalistic characterization of
Goldsmith's She Stoops to Conquer, though the
improbability of certain events makes it in her
opinion more like farce than comedy:

> She Stoops to Conquer has indeed
> more the quality of farce than of a
> regular, five-act drama: but, although
> some of the incidents are improbable,
> there is not one character in the piece,
> which is not perfectly in nature - The
> reader will find his country friends in
> the whole family of the Hardcastles; and,

most likely, one of his town acquaintances in the modest Mr. Marlow. - From the most severe judge, to the name of farce can be this comedy's sole reproach; and he must even then allow, that it is an extremely pleasant one; and a far better evening's entertainment, than the sentimental comedies of Kelly and other dramatists of that day - at which the auditors were never incited either to laugh or to cry.

Elizabeth often expresses, too, the specific point of view of a woman. of _Henry IV, Part I_ she writes:

This is a play which all men admire; and which most women dislike. Many revolting expressions in the comic parts, much boisterous courage in some of the graver scenes, together with Falstaff's unwieldy person, offend every female auditor; and whilst a facetious Prince of Wales is employed in taking purses on the highway, a lady would rather see him stealing hearts at a ball, though the event might produce more fatal consequences.

In her comments on Nathaniel Lee's _The Rival Queens_ she writes, very interestingly:

Dryden's Octavia is, however, much less refined than Lee's Statira. The first pardons her husband's love to Cleopatra, and is willing to accept his reluctant return, with an alienated heart;- whilst the last makes a solemn vow, never more to behold the man who loves her to distraction, because he has given her one proof of incontinence. There is deep knowledge of the female heart evinced in both these incidents. A woman is glad to be reconciled to the husband, who does not love her, upon any conditions - whilst the wife, who is beloved, is outrageous if she be not adored. Yet Lee should have considered, that such delicate expectations of perpetual constancy, as he has given to

his pagan queen, Statira, were not, so
late as his own time, prevalent, even
among Christian queens. The consorts of
Charles II and Louis XIV, saw as many
partakers of their royal spouses' love,
as the Sultana of Constantinople, and
with equal patience.

As a successful writer of comedy, she is
particularly concerned with its nature and with the
distinction between comedy, farce, comic opera, and
burlesque, the various forms of lighter
entertainment prevalent at the time. Of Arthur
Murphy's comedy, All in the Wrong, she writes:

> Molière's genius has been of use to
> many of our comic dramatists, who, at
> the time Mr. Murphy wrote, enriched
> their works with his wit and humour,
> without calling themselves translators,
> but merely occasional debtors to his
> primary invention .... The dialogue of
> All in the Wrong is of a species so
> natural, that it never in one sentence
> soars above the proper standard of
> elegant life; and the incidents that
> occur are bold without extravagance or
> apparent artifice, which is the
> criterion on which judgment should be
> formed between comedy and farce.

Broad farce she considered inelegant, as her
comments introducing George Colman the Younger's
comedy, John Bull, make clear:

> The irresistible broad humour,
> which is the predominant quality of this
> drama, is so exquisitely interspersed
> with touches of nature more refined,
> with occasional flashes of wit, and with
> events so interesting that, if the
> production is not of that perfect art
> which the most rigid critic demands, he
> must still acknowledge it is as a bond,
> given under the author's own hand, that
> he can, if he pleases, produce, in all
> its various branches, a complete comedy.

> The introduction of farces into the
> entertainments of the theatre has been

135

one cause of destroying that intimate
comedy, which such critics require. The
art which has been accustomed to delight
in painting of caricature, regards a
picture from real life as an insipid
work. The extravagance of farce has
given to the Town a taste for the
pleasant convulsion of big laughter, and
smiles are contemned as the token of
insipid amusement.

Comedy requires an exact judgment, acute
observation of manners, and above all the
elegancies of wit. Of Richard Cumberland's comedy,
The Brothers, she says:

> To give blunt repartee, or other
> humourous dialogue, to characters in low
> life; to produce variety of comic
> accidents, by which a petty tradesman, a
> sailor, or a country clown, shall raise
> a peal of laughter, is the easy
> attainment of every whimsical writer;
> but to exhibit the weak side of wisdom,
> the occasional foibles which impede the
> full exertion of good sense, the chance
> awkwardness of the elegant, and mistakes
> of the correct; to bestow wit on beauty,
> and to depict the passions, visible in
> the young, as well as in the aged; -
> these are efforts of intellect, required
> in the production of a good comedy, and
> can alone confer the title of a good
> comic author.

She also comments shrewdly on the basic
technical problem of adapting novels to the theatre
in the case of Colman the Younger, whose version of
Godwin's novel, Caleb Williams, retitled The Iron
Chest, she discussses:

> Narrative, on the stage, must never
> be diffuse; the play must be comprised
> in a certain number of pages; and, when
> the foundation of a fable is of the
> magnitude of murder, any abridgment of
> circumstances, requisite to make
> description both clear and probable,
> must be of fatal import to all the
> scenes so founded. British spectators of

a tragedy, moreover, even wish to behold the assassin's dagger reeking, before they listen to his groans of remorse; and the offence received, is sometimes demanded in exhibition, ere they will sympathize in the thirst of vengeance.

With all these values in mind, it is interesting to see which dramatists emerge best from Elizabeth's evaluation, always keeping in mind that the choice of the plays was predetermined for her. On Shakespeare she avoids offering much generalized comment, preferring in the main to quote Johnson, and relying specially on describing the effectiveness, or otherwise, of the key parts on the stage as played by Garrick, Kemble, Henderson, and others. As we have seen, she does not favor Romeo and Juliet because (she claims) it is not pleasing to an 'elegant audience,' and because what happens in the play strains credibility, as does the action in Cymbeline. Although the characterization in Henry IV, Part I is drawn from nature, the dialogue she finds offensive to genteel taste, whereas Henry V and Henry VIII are excellent precisely because they emphasize moral issues, as indeed, she says, does Macbeth. However, she singles out the acting parts which have proven most successful with audiences; though Garrick failed as Romeo, and as King John, he succeeded as Faulconbridge and Richard III; Henderson made a fine Falstaff, while Kemble was outstanding as Jaques, as the Duke in Measure for Measure, as Macbeth and Coriolanus, among many other Shakespearean parts.

She makes an interesting point about censorship affecting the final act of Richard III:

In the reign of William and Mary, the whole first act of this play was omitted in representation, by order of the licenser; who assigned as his reason - that the distresses of Henry VI, who is killed in the first act, by Richard, would put weak people too much in mind of King James II, who was then living an exile in France.

She speaks, too, about the censoring of certain lines from Coriolanus during the 1790s -

the key period of the revolution in France - since, 'certain sentences in this play are ... of dangerous tendency at certain times,' because of possible repercussion from 'the lower order of people.' However, the lines recently withheld have now been restored, she adds.

She comments, too, on the revisions imposed on Shakespeare's plays, especially in the case of King Lear:

> Tate alters the Play of King Lear, and instead of suffering the good Cordelia to die of grief, as Shakespeare had done, he rewards her with life, love, and a throne. Addison, in his Spectator, condemns him for this; Dr. Johnson commends him for it; Both showing excellent reasons. Then comes Steevens, who gives a better reason than all, why they are all wrong.[6]

Her character descriptions are often apt and clear. She speaks of King John's 'grovelling mind,' and of other Shakespearean characters, such as:

> Coriolanus: Here ... the likeness of a stubborn schoolboy, as well as of the obstinate general of an army, is so exquisitely delineated, that every mental trait of the one can be discerned in the propensities of the other, so as forcibly to call to the recollection, that children are the originals of man.

> Antony and Cleopatra: The reader will be also introduced to the queen of Egypt, in her undress, as well as in her royal robes; he will be, as it were, admitted to her toilet, where, in converse with her waiting-woman, she will suffer him to arrive at her most secret thoughts and designs: and he will quickly perceive, that the arts of a queen with her lover, are just the same as those practised by any other beauty - 'If you find Antony sad,' cries

Cleopatra, to her female attendant, 'say I am dancing; if he is in mirth, report that I am suddenly sick.'

These natural contrivances of artful woman, labouring to make her conquest and her power secure, are even outdone in truth of description, by that fretful impatience, with which she is tortured, in the absence of Antony from Egypt: By the gloom which the poet has spread throughout her whole palace, whilst he is away: and by the silly sentences, which, during this restless period, she is impelled to utter.

'Where think'st thou he is now? stands he, or sits he? Or does he walk? or is he on his horse?'

Silly sentences to all who never were in love, but sensible, and most intelligent to all who ever were.

Equal to the foregoing conversation, is that in which this impassioned queen makes anxious enquiry concerning the charms of her rival Octavia. But these minute touches of nature by which Shakespeare proves a queen to be a woman are, perhaps, the very cause why Dryden's picture of the Egyptian court is preferred on the stage before this. There are things so diminutive, they cannot be perceived in a theatre; whilst in a closet, their very smallness constitutes their value.

The Restoration dramatists represented here - Farquhar, Vanbrugh, and Congreve especially - trouble her. She responds to their talents as dramatists and dialogue writers, while she deplores the licentious indulgences their plays represent. Even severe adaptation cannot, she thinks, veil the immorality of the situations and motivations involved. She even castigates Gay's The Beggar's Opera, as we have seen. She does not appear to rate Beaumont and Fletcher, or for that matter Dryden, very highly as dramatists, while among the playwrights she considers to be too literary is Addison, whom she admires more as a Christian gentleman than as a dramatist. Moving nearer her own time, she is much more ready to admire the best work of Cibber, Rowe, Southerne, Lillo (the latter for originality), Goldsmith, Holcroft and the Colmans, though none escapes criticism when she feels this is due. Among women dramatists she praises Mrs. Centlivre (though decidedly not for the moral implications of her plays), Joanna Baillie, and to a lesser degree, Mrs. Cowley.

Her praise of Sheridan, the leading dramatist of wit and elegance in her time, is generous. She prefers The School for Scandal to The Rivals - the only play, apart from Sheridan's comic opera, The Duenna, the editors included in The British Theatre selection.

> The Rivals is an elegant, an interesting, a humorous, and most entertaining comedy; but in neither fable, character, nor incident, is it, like The School for Scandal - inimitable. If Mrs. Malaprop, Acres, Sir Lucius, and some other personages in this drama were not upon the stage before The Rivals was acted, they have all appeared there, in various dramas, many a time since. But where can Sir Peter and Lady Teazle, where can the Surface family be found, either in original or copy, except in The School for Scandal? Where can be traced the plot or events of that extraordinary play, or where even the shadows of them ....

> Sir Anthony Absolute is generally counted the most prominent, though Faulkland is, no doubt, the most original character in the comedy. One particular circumstance adds extreme interest to this part. It is supposed by the author's most intimate friends that, in delineating Faulkland, he took a discerning view of his own disposition, in all the anxious tenderness of a youthful lover; and has here accurately described every

sentiment, every feeling, which at that trying period of his life, agitated his troubled heart. The very town of Bath, just before the writing of this play, had been the identical scene of all his restless hopes and fears.

The impressive language, the refined notions, the enthusiastic, yet natural passion of Faulkland for Julia, with all the captivating charms of mind and expression which has been here given to this object of adoration, are positive vouchers that some very exalted idea of the force of love, if not its immediate power over himself, had at that time possession of the poet's fancy.

Elizabeth does not approve of the character of Mrs. Malaprop, and addresses us directly in the 20th century when dealing with her:

Against the illiterate Mrs. Malaprop, common occurrence and common sense protest. That any Englishwoman, for these five hundred years past, in the habit of keeping good company, or any company, could have made use of the words - extirpate for exculpate, exhort for escort, and malevolence for benevolence - seems too far removed from probability to make a reasonable auditor smile.

When future generations shall naturally suppose that an author of Mr. Sheridan's reputation drew men and women exactly as he found them; this sketch of a woman of family and fortune, at the end of the eighteenth century, will assure the said generations that the advance of female knowledge in Great Britain was far more tardy than in any other European nation.

Occasionally, plays out of the ordinary offer her opportunities for comment on unconventional subjects. George Barnwell, or The London Merchant (1731), George Lillo's tragedy based on a popular ballad, represented for her a 'new species of

141

pathetic drama.' The author of this tragedy was a tradesman,' she writes, 'which might influence his taste for the description of scene of humble life.' She traces the ups and downs in favor that this tragedy in prose about humble people experienced with audiences used only to witnessing the destructive passions of the great. She holds Lillo in high regard, and quotes Fielding's commendation of him as a man, written when he died in 1739. Then again, the opera, <u>Inkle and Yarico</u>, by George Colman the Younger opened up, like Southerne's <u>Oroonoko</u>, the subject of slavery. Of this she says:

> This opera was written, when the author was very young, and, should he live to be very old, he will have reason to be proud of it to his latest day, for it is one of those plays which is independent of time, of place, or of circumstance, for its value. It was popular before the subject of the abolition of the slave trade was popular. It has the peculiar honour of preceding that great question. It was the bright forerunner of alleviation to the hardships of slavery.

Similarly, Richard Cumberland's <u>The Jew</u> (1794) introduced a subject hitherto absent in the English theatre, where Jews were normally seen by tradition as either villains or comic characters, as in <u>The Jew of Malta</u> and <u>The Merchant of Venice</u>. Elizabeth comments:

> When a zealous Christian writes in favour of a Jew, it is proof of the truest christianity. The author of this play has done more than befriend one unfortunate descendant of Abraham; he has taken the twelve tribes of Israel under his protection. The bravery of this enterprise was equal to its charity – the execution has been masterly – and complete success the reward of that compassion which incited him to his labour .... The play, in its formation, is adverse to the public taste, and in its sentiments contrary to public prejudice; still the public were charmed

with it.

Finally, it is natural she should take constant pleasure in describing actors at work. Impressions of acting are peculiarly difficult to reconstruct for readers who have never seen the original performer, but Elizabeth is never afraid to try. Her recollection of the Kemble-Siddons production of <u>Macbeth</u> at the Theatre Royal, Drury Lane, inspires her:

> To those who are unacquainted with the effect wrought by theatrical action and decoration, it may not be superfluous to say - the huge rocks, the enormous caverns, and blasted heaths of Scotland, in the scenery; the highland warrior's dress, of centuries past, worn by the soldiers and their generals; the splendid robes and banquet at the royal court held at Fores; the awful, yet inspiring music which accompanies words assimilated to each sound; and above all, the fear, the terror, the remorse; the agonizing throbs and throes, which speak in looks, whispers, sudden starts, and writhings, by Kemble and Mrs. Siddons, all tending to one great precept - <u>Thou shalt not murder</u>.

Above all, she enjoys celebrating John Philip Kemble, whose performances shine again through the energy of her prose, and span the whole series of volumes. He excels, she claims, in Shakespeare, being second only to Garrick, to whose genius as an actor she frequently refers, for example, his Gloucester in <u>Richard III</u>:

> Garrick, Henderson, Kemble, and Cooke, have all in their turn been favoured with the love, as well as the admiration of the town for acting Richard .... Garrick appears to have been the actor, of all others, best suited for this character. His diminutive figure gave the best personal likeness of the crooked-back king. He had, besides, if tradition may be relied

on, the first abilities as a mimic; and
Richard himself was a mass of mimicry,
except in his ambition and his cruelty.

Among the many parts to which she makes
special reference in describing Kemble is his
performance as the King in King John:

> The part of King John is held most
> difficult to perform. John is no hero,
> and yet he is a murderer; his best
> actions are debased by meanness, deceit,
> or cowardice, and yet he is a king.
> Here is then to be portrayed, thirst of
> blood, without thirst of fame; and
> dignity of person, with a groveling mind
> .... The genius of Kemble gleams
> terrific through the gloomy John. No
> auditor can hear him call for his
>
> 'Kingdom's rivers to take their course
> Through his burn'd bosom,'
>
> and not feel for that moment parched
> with a scorching fever.

As we have seen, she praises his performance in
Macbeth and among other Shakespearean roles:

> Of Jaques in As You Like It:
> Kemble's Jaques is in the highest
> estimation with the public: it is one
> of those characters in which he gives
> certain bold testimonies of genius,
> which no spectator can controvert. Yet
> the mimic art has very little share in
> this grand exhibition.
>
> Of Coriolanus: Kemble 'renders the
> utmost summit of the actor's art.'

As for other plays than Shakespeare's, she admires
especially his work

> As Osmyn in Congreve's The Mourning
> Bride: Kemble looks nobly,
> majestically, in Osmyn, and reminds the
> audience of the lines,
>
> - Tall pillar rear its marble head,

144

Looking tranquility ....
And shoots a chillness to the trembling
heart.

As Zanga in Young's parallel to
Shakespeare's Othello, The Revenge:
This character is of such magnitude, and
so unprotected by those who surround
him, that few performers will undertake
to represent it; a less number still
have succeeded in braving the danger.
Mr. Kemble stands foremost among those,
and draws some splendid audiences every
year, merely to see him, though the
intervals between his exits and
entrances are sure to be passed in
lassitude.

The many introductions for The British
Theatre series were to be the only substantial
undertaking in dramatic or literary criticism
Elizabeth was to publish. In doing so, in the
earliest years of the 19th century, she established
professional standards for the woman critic that
had no previous parallel. In particular, her
comments were valuable because they revealed in
virtually every instance the knowledge and
experience of an actress who over a number of years
had enjoyed the privilege of working with and
observing at the closest range the performances of
the best players of the time, not now and then but
on hundreds of occasions, behind the scenes and on
the stage, as participant and as member of an
audience in the theatres of London and the
provinces.

Painted by Lawrence – Engraved by Freeman.

Mrs Inchbald.

Published by Vernor, Hood & Sharpe, Poultry, July 1.1807.

Elizabeth Inchbald
From an undated original painting

V

THE LAST YEARS

Elizabeth spent the final ten years or more of her life in semi-retirement from the writing that had by 1810 brought her sufficient money on which to live in parsimonious comfort. She endured indifferent health during her mid-fifties, and was to survive to the age of 67 (or 68 according to the inscription on her tomb),[1] dying on 1 August 1821. She never cured herself of wandering from place to place in the London area, living now in the heart of London, now on its outskirts. Around 1800 she was residing in rooms in Leicester Fields (Leicester Square) - she refers in a letter of this period to 'going up and down three pair of long stairs with water or dirt,' and finishing 'scouring my bedchamber, while a coach with a coronet and two footmen waited at the door to take me an airing.'[2] But she wrote to her closest friend, Mrs. Phillips of Suffolk, in the summer of 1802, 'Leicester Square is so beautiful! from the vast rains it is green as in the spring! and London so still, at least to me, that I am certain I surpass you in solitude.' She left here, however, in the summer of the following year to live in Annandale House in Turnham Green, a community of Catholic gentlewomen. This was not in the end successful, and she left to live again in central London, securing lodgings in the Strand at the very top of a house which commanded a view over the Thames to the Surrey Hills beyond, with three large windmills in sight. But this apartment proved too small - 'I am all over black and blue with thumping my body and limbs against my furniture on every side.' By 1810 she moved herself and her furniture to commodious, first floor rooms in St. George's Row, looking over Hyde Park - but here she had trouble with the landlord, who misrepresented his ownership of the property. She loved living in London and was determined not to quit it:

> The scene is more beautiful than
> ever. The trees tipt with golden
> leaves, and the canal peeping through

their branches, which are half stript,
with the grass of the extensive ground
as green as in Spring, all delight my
eye and almost break my heart. I must
have <u>London</u>, combined with the sun, the
moon, and the stars, with land and with
water, to fill my imagination, and
excite my contemplation.[3]

She suffered from the cold in St. George's Row -
the winter always caused her to catch severe colds
as a result of inadequate heating, to which she
seemed condemned. She moved in May 1811 to another
house in the same terrace, but quit this in 1816
for lodgings in Earl's Terrace, opposite Holland
House, Kensington. She dreaded these removals; she
wrote to Mrs. Phillips:

My spirits were so low that day, I
came out for society; but not to eat;
for I have not eat since I knew of my
destined removal. Such a horror I have
of packing my trunks and furniture - of
seeing new faces, and hearing <u>new</u>
voices, with <u>old</u> observations, that I
never leave one lodging for another,
without wishing myself in jail for debt,
without the benefit of an insolvent act.[4]

But Earl's Terrace did not last for long
either. In October 1818 she moved to other
lodgings in Sloane Street, an area she professed to
dislike. Finally, in April 1819 she moved to a
large, well-managed establishment at Kensington
House, where she remained until she died of her
last illness.

Her financial circumstances caused her no
fundamental worry. Her publishers were to change
(Longmans succeeding Robinsons), but her finances
were sound owing to the thrifty way in which she
had invested her money, the capital sums she
received from her plays. She never converted her
basic capital into an annuity, which would have
greatly increased her income, this it would seem
out of concern for her heirs.[5] Her income appears
to have been about 170 pounds a year, and when she
died she left capital of some 5,000 pounds, a sum
approximately equal to the total of her earnings
from her plays.

Her only literary preoccupation in her later years was her <u>Memoirs</u>, which were constantly being revised and read for advice by her friends and for consideration by potential publishers. Almost all other writing she rejected, worn out by the effort required to compile her various prefaces to her first collection of plays, <u>The British Theatre</u>. She also abandoned the translation of Corneille's plays into prose, work she had begun in 1807. When in December 1808 she was approached to contribute to the <u>Quarterly Review</u>, newly established in London, she declined. In 1809-11 she put her name to two collections of plays, <u>The Modern Theatre</u> and <u>Collection of Farces and Afterpieces</u>, but she wrote no prefaces to them. She was offered the editorship of John Bell's magazine, <u>La Belle Assemblée</u>, but all she wrote was an occasional essay - one on the novel, for instance, for publication in <u>The Artist</u>[6] - and her constant output of letters, many preserved and quoted by Boaden.

The <u>Memoirs</u>, however, had remained of some concern to her. She had been encouraged initially to write these by Robinson. Boaden quotes an undated letter of around 1802 which shows something of the interest the prospect of these memoirs excited:

> The maid came up the other day and said Mr. Phillips was below, and wished to speak to me on business, if I was alone. I ran to the door, 'Pray walk in, Mr. Phillips.' A tall, black-looking, vulgar man entered. I was astonished; it was Phillips, the bookseller, of St. Paul's Churchyard - a total stranger to me. He came to offer me a thousand pounds for my 'Life,' without wishing to read a line of it beforehand. This summer I shall sit in judgment on it and decide.'[7]

When the manuscript had reached a stage of completion, she began to submit it to the judgment of such friends as Hardinge. Boaden writes:

> Her heart (no wonder) was with the Robinson house; and they agreed to buy, if they liked the work on perusal. It

was returned, with a letter from Mr.
Chalmers, which seems to have, for the
time at least, suspended the desire to
publish. However, though she did not
send for Phillips and take his thousand
pounds, she went again to work upon them
in the way of alteration and addition,
and submitted her 'Memoirs' to the
judgment of Mr. Hardinge and her new
friends, Dr. and Mrs. Moody. When she
was spoken to by her female friends in
the theatre, as to publication, she used
to assume a look of terror, and exclaim,
'Would you have me mur-dered?' - all
well enough calculated to keep up an
excitement upon the subject; but she
would have destroyed herself with her
fashionable friends, if her work really
were of so alarming a cast.[8]

He adds, commenting on the year 1804, that she made
'more additions to her "Life,"' adding, 'How she
treated her fashionable friends, we can only
imagine; if she intended to live in the same set
after publication, she must have greatly curbed her
caustic sincerity .... The love of money was always
strong in her.'[9] Robinson, however, refused to
publish the book on her terms.

John Taylor, in his Records of my Life, has
an amusing passage about the Memoirs:

The manuscript was submitted to the
judgment of my friend Mr. Alexander
Chalmers, and a more liberal and
judicious critic could not have been
found. As the work consisted chiefly of
that portion of her life which passed in
provincial theatrical companies, before
she came to London, and nothing of what
occurred after she was engaged at a
London theatre, when her mind was
expanded, and her knowledge augmented by
an intercourse with literary and other
enlightened connexions, Mr. Chalmers
advised her to suppress it, and she
submitted to his opinion, though she was
then in narrow circumstances. She did
not, however, destroy the manuscript. A
popular publisher of that time hearing of

the work, waited on her, and offered one hundred pounds for it. She referred him to Mr. Chalmers .... 'Oh!,' said Mr. Chalmers, 'if you imagine it contains anything that the chastest eye ought not to peruse, you are grossly mistaken.' Hearing these words, the publisher started from his chair, seized his hat, left the room abruptly, and hurried to Mrs. Inchbald, telling her that he declined purchasing the work.[10]

When in 1805 Longmans took over as her publisher from Robinsons (the firm had gone bankrupt), they too proved cautious about publishing the Memoirs; later another publisher, Constable, also declined it, and Boaden implies that by this time she herself was tired of the constant revisions and trimmings to which the script had been subjected during the period its publication had been under consideration. She ordered the destruction of the manuscript at her death, and it was burnt.[11]

Her life from around 1810 became a matter of preoccupation with her constant round of social visits, both inside and outside London, serious attention to her health, which worried her and involved increasingly severe colds caught during the winter, and her continuous concern about where and how to live on her very limited income. Some close friends and relatives died, and were in certain cases a special loss to her. Her stepson, George Inchbald, whom she had on occasion helped financially, died in October 1800, while Robert Inchbald (the boy Bob of the period of her marriage) became a great nuisance to her in her later years, always causing trouble and pestering her for money. Her sister, Mrs. Bigsby, had died in 1799, and her brother, Edward Simpson, in 1805. Her somewhat ill-tempered and irresponsible sister, Dolly, often ill and in need of help, died suddenly in 1809.

Among her friends, Holcroft died also in 1809, but worst of all, perhaps, her beloved Dr. Warren had died as early as 1797. Elizabeth had felt moved to commemorate his loss in verse, which she sent to his widow; this is notable, because she always claimed she could not write poetry:

151

Death is the doom of man - yet must we grieve
That one of wisdom sure, of high renown,
Of skill the pangs of others to relieve,
So soon should fall a victim to his own.

Yet must we worth lament which all would prize
If all had known; and chant the prouder claim
To talents, of such excellence, and size,
That envy shrunk, and dared not to defame.

Nor stop we here, nor be his praise confined
To depth of science, or superior art:
No - the strong spring of his sagacious mind
Was ruled and temper'd by a feeling heart.

Hence doth his fame-though much to that be due
Not on his health-restoring skill depend,
The splendid actor shone in every view,
As husband, father, relative, and friend.[12]

Thereafter, her health had become the care of Dr.
Phillips, husband of her close friend, the Mrs.
Phillips who was to be her executor. Mrs. Phillips
had taken care of Mrs. Bigsby during her last days,
and Elizabeth's letter of gratitude to her is
indicative not only of her conscienciousness, but
her strict sense of economy:

> I am more apt than most people to
> start at expense, but believe me 'tis
> only when I witness expenses that are
> superfluous. Upon an occasion like the
> present, with you for the manager of my
> purse, I shall consider every farthing
> expended as indispensably necessary, and
> from my heart rejoice that I have earned
> and saved a little money for so good a
> purpose.
>
> I have no one direction to give
> you, because you perfectly understand my
> wishes - everything requisite to the
> comfort and decency of her and those
> about her, and nothing further. I will
> add, it would be more satisfactory if
> the weekly expenses, after you come
> away, could be ascertained; and that no
> bill of any kind should be run on her
> account, but an immediate demand sent to
> me, or an immediate statement of any

152

thing taken up on an emergency. I do
this, to preserve myself from the
temptation of thinking I have been
imposed on by unnecessary expenses, and
a kind of selfish surprise, which too
frequently accompanies the receipt of
the most just bill.[13]

Some of Elizabeth's best, most humane letters
were written by her to Mrs. Phillips.[14]

Elizabeth read as much as she could, joining
a circulating library which charged her as little
as eight shillings and sixpence a quarter and
allowed her as many as four books at a time. A
young friend, Miss Marlow, in a letter sent after
Elizabeth's death to Mrs. Phillips, said that
'whenever I did call, she appeared so overwhelmed
with reading and business, that I always felt it an
intrusion.'[15] However, it appears Elizabeth began
to regret she had never had a child, and, around
1801, felt a kind of maternal love for the infant
son of her landlord of the time. She wrote:

The only thing which I can at
present think of, which you will not
probably read in a newspaper, is that I
lament more than ever I did the not
having had a child. I was always fond
of children, but, till of late, I never
paid any attention to them till they
could speak. A child was born in this
house last October, and I, having seen
it every day since that time, have been
so enchanted by its increasing beauty
and sense, that, though I have not the
smallest acquaintance with either of its
parents, I think I love it almost better
than any thing in the world. A child of
this age is the most curious thing I
ever met with; the most entertaining and
the most affectionate.[16]

Elizabeth also interested herself in the
career of Sarah Siddons' young son, Henry, who
appeared as Hamlet at Covent Garden late in 1801,
in connection with which the following letter,
dated 11 October 1802, survives:

Mr. Harris has just left me, the

first time I have seen him since your son performed: he has requested me to convey to you his sincerest thanks for the very great acquisition you have rendered to Covent Garden theatre by the recommendation of so valuable an actor.

It may appear strange to you that I should have a commission of this kind from Mr. Harris, but he sometimes honours me with his confidence; and having this morning communicated to me the very high value he places upon his new performer, I was so sincerely delighted that I believe he thought it would gratify me to fulfill the task he then set me.

Do not imagine that I had not formed my opinion of Harry's abilities before I knew what Mr. Harris's was; but a manager's opinion can frequently counteract those of a whole town, and it is difficult even for dramatic <u>genius</u> to bear up against a dissatisfied employer. On this account I tell you of the manager's high estimation of your son with a peculiar pleasure, though it has not in the least augmented my own.[17]

Living in London, she went often to the theatre, and her comments on the infatuation London audiences felt in 1804 for the child actor, Master Betty, the young Roscius as he was called, were caustic.[18] Since he was to appear in a play of hers, <u>Lovers' Vows</u>, she was forced to take some note of him. She first saw him in company with the Kembles, watching from their box at Covent Garden:

I have avoided giving my opinion of young Betty, because I am by no means confident it is a right one. I hate all <u>prodigies</u> - partly, I fancy, because I have no faith in them. Under this prejudice I saw his first performance, and was so disgusted by a monotony, a preaching-like tone, that I gave up my place at the end of the third act, and walked behind the scenes, where myriads of critics were gathered, to listen to

154

their remarks. Here some vociferated that Garrick was returned to the stage .... But as all that is said for him is in a <u>loud</u> voice, and all against him in a <u>low</u> one, praise must go forth and criticism be scarcely heard. Indeed, on returning to my seat in the fifth act, I found he had great spirit, great fire in the impassioned scenes, which gave variety to his tones, and made me say, 'This is a clever little boy,' and, had I never seen boys act, I might have thought him extraordinary.

The next night I liked him better, in my own play, <u>Lovers' Vows</u>; he was more natural and more spirited, though he totally mistook the passion in his best scene - still he gave <u>a</u> passion, though not the right one; and the audience were charmed .... This boy is one of the reasons for my selling my play .... Such is the rage of the multitude, that a new play even from Shakespeare could hardly contend against him.[19]

Elizabeth maintained her close friendship with Kemble. In 1802-3 she had negotiated the purchase of one-sixth part of the patent for Covent Garden theatre on Kemble's behalf during his absence in Spain and France. She was on friendly terms with Mrs. Priscilla Kemble, at some periods dining with her and her husband on Sundays, at other periods cooling somewhat towards them. On one occasion in June, 1811, Kemble, in boisterous mood, abducted her for dinner, as she wrote in excuse to Mrs. Phillips, with whom she should have dined:

I hope you were not angry that I did not come to dinner last Sunday; nor will be, when I tell you that I dined out. It was my full intention to have come to you, though I did not hold myself <u>pledged</u>; but the day was so extremely warm, and I so fatigued with lighting my fire, and other very warm household work, that I had just concluded it was impossible for me to

155

walk to Pall Mall, and very improbable I could hire a coach, - when Mr. Kemble called with his carriage, and forced me to ascend from my own door into it. You may remember I told you I had been invited there on that day, but had sent a refusal. He would not be refused.[20]

Kemble was only to retire from the stage in 1817, and in 1820 leave England permanently to live in Switzerland on the death of his partner, Harris. Elizabeth was never to see him again. Godwin, too, maintained some kind of contact with her, though she persisted in keeping him at arm's length. But some letters survive; for example, Godwin saw Kemble in To Marry or not to Marry in 1805, and wrote to her on 18 February:

I congratulate you on your success of Saturday night, which I witnessed with much pleasure. Kemble scarcely ever appeared to so much advantage: you inspired him, and he understood you.[21]

Or again, on 1 December, 1817:

I cannot appear before the world in my old character of a novelist without recollecting with some emotion the sort of intercourse that passed between us when Caleb Williams was in his non-age, and in the vigor of his age. Particularly, I have looked a hundred times with great delight at the little marginal notes and annotations with which you adorned the pages of my writings of that period. Do me the favour to read Mandeville with some recollections of the time I allude to; and if, when you have gone through it, you will oblige me so far as to return the copy with your remarks, I will request your acceptance of a fresh one in exchange for it.[22]

On December 23, Godwin wrote to her again giving some account of the publisher Constable's admiration for her, though the work referred to in his letter, Elizabeth's Memoirs, was not in the end accepted by him for publication:

Mr. Constable has flown with the eagerness of a lover to the perusal of your MS, at every moment he could rescue from the remorseless gripe of business. I never saw a man so fascinated. I believe, the instant I leave his apartment at any time, he takes up the book and kisses it. He says he never saw an MS so beautiful: you best know whether, in so saying, he alludes to the elegance of the penmanship, or the charms of the narrative. Mr. Constable is a widower, of an amorous complexion, and I am not sure that he has not been guilty of the indelicacy of having endeavoured to prevail on the book to come to bed with him. Do not therefore be hard-hearted, and refuse to admit the man into your presence who thus worships your image.[23]

Godwin had in fact accompanied Constable on a visit to Elizabeth when she had loaned him the script.

Among her staunchest male friends was John Taylor, distinguished journalist, proprietor and editor of The Sun. In his Records of my Life (1832), he wrote: 'I became acquainted with this lady in the year 1782, and an uninterrupted friendship existed between us till her death,'[24] and adds he was in the habit of visiting her every Sunday morning for many years. He also recollects that he warned her, out of friendship, that people thought she was not only miserly but insane to live in the manner she did. Her reply is specially revealing, written when she was 52 and living in the Strand:

Because I choose that retirement suitable to my years, and think it my duty to support two sisters, instead of one servant, I am accused of madness. I might plunge in debt, be confined in prison, a pensioner on 'The Literary Fund,' or be gay as a girl of eighteen, and yet be considered as perfectly in my senses; but because I choose to live in independence, affluence to me, with a mind serene and prospects unclouded, I am supposed to be mad .... Retirement in

the country would, perhaps, have been
more advisable than in London, but my
sisters did not like to accompany me,
and I did not like to leave them
behind. There is, besides, something
animating in the reflection that I am in
London .... Much as it is supposed that
I value money, I would gladly give up
all I am at present earning, and
something added to it, that I had never
engaged in those unwieldy Prefaces. I
have had my Memoirs, in four volumes,
for years lying by me. A large sum has
been offered for them, yet, though I am
charged with loving money, I never
hesitated when I conceived that my
reputation was in the balance. I
accepted the offer made to me to write
these things as far the less evil of the
two, indeed as no evil; but now I fear
that I should not have encountered more
odium had I published my life.[25]

Once, when he asked her why she had not married
again, she said, 'That for wedlock, friendship was
too familiar, and love too precarious.' Taylor,
too, was among the friends to whom she showed her
tragedy, The Massacre, with a note attached:

I am undetermined whether to
publish this play or not - do, dear
creature, give me your opinion. I will
send for an answer tomorrow, or if you
call here, leave a note if I am from
home.[26]

'As far as I recollect,' adds Taylor, 'I advised
her to suppress it.'

A letter of 19 May, 1918, survives in MS at
the Victoria and Albert Museum in London, and shows
how warmly Elizabeth felt towards Taylor; she is
offering him fifty pounds when he is in financial
difficulties, a sum which Boaden says she
subsequently gave him.

If during the various claims upon
you in your professional concerns the
little sum of fifty pounds can ever
within this half year, be of the

slighest service to you, send me a note,
only one day before you call for it, and
I will have it ready to deliver into
your hands without making you wait a
moment - not even to write a memorandum
- for never shall I wish to think of it
again. - At present I expend upon my
maintenance the whole of my yearly
income, including four pounds now and
then to a nephew, an unsuccessful and
indigent farmer. - But I have hoarded
twenty golden guineas and twenty-nine
one pound notes, in case I should return
to London and once more have to furnish
lodgings. - But these views have changed
of late and I have almost fixed to
continue where I am - at all events do
not despise my humble offer if it can be
of the least use to you, for if it can,
no one purchase I could make would give
me half the satisfaction as this puny
testimony of your long and zealous
exertions towards my welfare. I am,
Living or Dying, most gratefully yours,
Eliz. Inchbald.[27]

Another friendship of interest and importance
was that which sprang up with Maria Edgeworth and
her devoted family - her Irish father, Richard
Lovell Edgeworth, and her two brothers, Sneyd and
Lovell. Maria and her father, an educationalist,
had co-authored Practical Education (1798), which
was much influenced by Rousseau, while Maria's
Irish novel, Castle Rackrent, had appeared in
1800. Both father and daughter wrote
enthusiastically to Elizabeth. In January 1810,
Elizabeth received the following letter in praise
of A Simple Story from Maria, who at 43 years of
age was 14 years junior to Elizabeth:

I hope you will not suspect me of
the common author practice of returning
praise for praise, when I tell you that
I have just been reading, for the third
- I believe for the fourth time - the
'Simple Story.' Its effect upon my
feelings was as powerful as at the first
reading; I never read any novel - I
except none - I never read any novel
that affected me so strongly, or that so

159

completely possessed me with the belief in the real existence of all the people it represents. I never once recollected the author whilst I was reading it; never said or thought, <u>that's a fine sentiment</u> - or, <u>that is well expressed</u> - or <u>that is well invented</u>. I believed all to be real, and was affected as I should be by the real scenes if they had passed before my eyes; it is truly and deeply pathetic. I determined, this time of reading, to read it as a critic - or rather, as an author, to try to find out the secret of its peculiar pathos. But I quite forgot my intention in the interest Miss Milner and Dorriforth excited; but <u>now it is all over</u>, and that I can coolly exercise my judgment, I am of opinion that it is by leaving more than most other writers to the imagination, that you succeed so eminently in affecting it. By the force that is necessary to repress feeling, we judge of the intensity of the feeling; and you always contrive to give us by intelligible but simple signs the measure of this force. Writers of inferior genius waste their words in <u>describing</u> feeling; in making those who pretend to be agitated by passion describe the effects of that passion, and talk of the <u>rending of their hearts, etc</u>. A gross blunder! as gross as any Irish blunder; for the heart cannot feel, and describe its own feelings, at the same moment. It is <u>'being like a bird in two places at once</u> .... Did you really draw the characters from life? or did you invent them? You excel, I think, peculiarly in avoiding what is commonly called <u>fine writing</u> - a sort of writing which I detest; which calls the attention away from the <u>thing</u> to the <u>manner</u> - from the feeling to the language; which sacrifices every thing to sound, to the mere rounding of a period; which mistakes <u>stage effect</u> for <u>nature</u>. All who are at all used to writing, know and detect the <u>trick of the trade</u> immediately; and, speaking for

160

myself, I <u>know</u> that the writing which has least the appearance of literary <u>manufacture</u> almost always pleases me the best. It has more originality; in narration of fictitious events, it most surely succeeds in giving the idea of reality, and in making the biographer, for the time, pass for nothing. But there are few who can in this manner bear the <u>mortification</u> of staying behind the scenes. They peep out, eager for applause, and destroy all illusion by crying, 'I said it; I wrote it; I invented it all! Call me on the stage and crown me directly.'[28]

Boaden prints a letter from Maria's father which shows an equal enthusiasm for <u>A Simple Story</u>, while Maria's desire to meet Elizabeth shines in another, undated letter:

Your letters, like your books, are so original, so interesting, and give me so much the idea of truth and reality, that I am more and more desirous to be personally acquainted with you; ....
There are some authors whose books make so much the best part of them, that one can think of nothing else in writing to them; but in writing to Mrs. Inchbald, I can at this moment think of nothing but the wish to see <u>her</u>, and to enjoy her society.[29]

Maria was constantly and earnestly to seek Elizabeth's opinion on all the work she produced, but it would seem they did not meet until 1813, the year in which Elizabeth was to encounter Mme. de Staël, introduced to her by another of her friends, Mrs. Opie.[30] Mme. de Staël was then one of the foremost women writers of the time, and on a visit to London. A woman of great intellectual gifts, she represented the highly independent, liberated woman of the period. Elizabeth left some account of this meeting in 1813 in a letter to Mrs. Phillips, under a significant title that actually (though obviously humorously) identified herself with the heroine of <u>A Simple Story</u>:

MEETING BETWEEN 'CORINNE' AND MISS MILNER.

I will now mention the calamity of a neighbour, by many degrees the first female writer in the world, as she is called by the Edinburgh Reviewers. Madame de Staël asked a lady of my acquaintance to introduce her to me. The lady was our mutual acquaintance, of course, and so far my friend as to conceal my place of abode; yet she menaced me with a visit from the Baroness of Holstein, if I would not consent to meet her at a third house. After much persuasion, I did so. I admired Madame de Staël much; she talked to me the whole time; so did Miss Edgeworth whenever I met her in company. These authoresses suppose me dead, and seem to pay a tribute to my memory; but with Madame de Staël it seemed no passing compliment; she was inquisitive as well as attentive, and entreated me to explain to her the motive why I shunned society? 'Because,' I replied, 'I dread the loneliness that will follow.' 'What! will you feel your solitude more when you return from this company, than you did before you came hither?' 'Yes.' 'I should think it would elevate your spirits: why will you feel your loneliness more?' 'Because I have no one to tell that I have seen you; no one to describe your person to; no one to whom I can repeat the many encomiums you have passed on my "Simple Story;" no one to enjoy any of your praises but myself.' 'Ah, ah! you have no children:' and she turned to an elegant young woman, her daughter, with pathetic tenderness. She then so forcibly depicted a mother's joys, that she sent me home more melancholy at the comparison of our situations in life, than could have arisen from the consequences of riches or poverty.[31]

Elizabeth's last years, therefore, were by no

means those of a recluse, in spite of her recurrent
ill-health and her lack of means to lead other than
a hard life without the help of a servant. She was
nevertheless undoubtedly lonely. Samuel Rogers,
the well-known man-about-town as well as man of
letters and versification, recalls a meeting with
her in his Table Talk:

> Not long before Mrs. Inchbald died,
> I met her walking near Charing Cross.
> She told me that she had been calling on
> several old friends, but had seen none
> of them - some being really not at home,
> and others denying themselves to her.
> 'I called,' she said, 'on Mrs. Siddons.
> I knew she was at home; yet I was not
> admitted.' She was in such low spirits
> that she shed tears. I begged her to
> turn with me, and take a quiet dinner at
> St. James Place, but she refused.[32]

Perhaps it was a bad day, and she felt alone and
indisposed. In her own words, however, she
cherished the quieter life she was able to live in
her later years. She said as much to Mrs. Phillips
as early as November 1808:

> As to myself, I have had my full
> share of the world - a busy share from
> fifteen to fifty. I should want taste
> did I not now enjoy that variety in life
> which I gain by solitude .... I had five
> of almost continual loneliness and
> quiet;- extreme justified only by
> necessity .... Do not suppose you can
> alarm me by representing the state of
> APATHY as a calamity. It is the
> BLESSING of old age; it is the
> substitute for patience. It permits me
> to look in the glass without screaming
> with horror - and to live upon moderate
> terms of charity with all young people
> (without much hatred or malice),
> although I can never be young again.[33]

Boaden also stresses that she turned with greater
regularity than in the past to the Catholic Church
for solace. He writes: 'From the year 1777 to
this very year 1810 she had called her religious
existence NOTHING .... She calls the rest of her

163

life years of repentance.' Her design, he says of
her again in 1812, was 'to reconcile herself
entirely with her Church.'[34]

There is no better way to end this
appreciation of Elizabeth Inchbald than with her
own self-description (or perhaps self-depreciation)
written in middle life in the same half-caustic,
half-amused tone so characteristic of her subtle
mingling of wit and humor:

DESCRIPTION OF ME

AGE –	Between 30 and 40, which, in the register of a lady's birth, means a little turned of 30.
HEIGHT –	Above the middle size, and rather tall.
FIGURE –	Handsome, and striking in its general air, but a little too stiff and erect.
SHAPE –	Rather too fond of sharp angles.
SKIN –	By nature fair, though a little freckled, and with a tinge of sand, which is the colour of her eye-lashes, but made coarse by ill-treatment upon her cheeks and arms.
BOSOM –	None; or so diminutive, that it's like a needle in a bottle of hay.
HAIR –	Of a sandy auburn, and rather too straight as well as thin.
FACE –	Beautiful in effect, and beautiful in every feature.
COUNTENANCE –	Full of spirit and sweetness; excessively interesting, and, without indelicacy, voluptuous.
DRESS –	Always becoming; and very seldom worth so much as eight-pence.[35]

To this can only be added what John Genest said by
way of commendation:

        She was little inferior to any of
her contemporaries, and very superior to
most of them.[36]

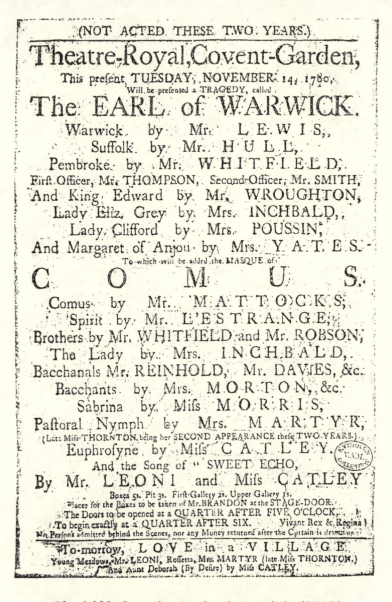

(NOT ACTED THESE TWO YEARS.)

Theatre-Royal, Covent-Garden,

This present TUESDAY, NOVEMBER 14, 1780,
Will be presented a TRAGEDY, called

The EARL of WARWICK.

Warwick by Mr. L E W I S,
Suffolk by Mr. H U L L,
Pembroke by Mr. W H I T F I E L D,
First Officer, Mr. THOMPSON, Second Officer, Mr. SMITH,
And King Edward by Mr. WROUGHTON,
Lady Eliz. Grey by Mrs. INCHBALD,
Lady Clifford by Mrs. POUSSIN,
And Margaret of Anjou by Mrs. Y A T E S.
To which will be added the MASQUE of

C O M U S.

Comus by Mr. M A T T O C K S,
Spirit by Mr. L'E S T R A N G E,
Brothers by Mr. WHITFIELD and Mr. ROBSON,
The Lady by Mrs. I N C H B A L D,
Bacchanals Mr. REINHOLD, Mr. DAVIES, &c.
Bacchants by Mrs. M O R T O N, &c.
Sabrina by Miss M O R R I S,
Pastoral Nymph by Mrs. M A R T Y R,
(Late Miss THORNTON, being her SECOND APPEARANCE these TWO YEARS.)
Euphrosyne by Miss C A T L E Y.
And the Song of " SWEET ECHO,
By Mr. L E O N I and Miss C A T L E Y

Boxes 5s. Pit 3s. First Gallery 2s. Upper Gallery 1s.
Places for the Boxes to be taken of Mr. BRANDON at the STAGE-DOOR.
The Doors to be opened at a QUARTER AFTER FIVE O'CLOCK,
To begin exactly at a QUARTER AFTER SIX. Vivant Rex & Regina
No Persons admitted behind the Scenes, nor any Money returned after the Curtain is drawn up

To-morrow, L O V E in a V I L L A G E
Young Meadows, Mr. LEONI, Rosetta, Mrs. MARTYR (late Miss THORNTON,)
And Aunt Deborah (By Desire) by Miss CATLEY.

Playbill for The Earl of Warwick (1780)
at Theatre Royal, Covent Garden,
with Elizabeth Inchbald as
Lady Elizabeth Grey, and for Comus,
with Elizabeth Inchbald as The Lady
(Enthoven Collection,
Victoria and Albert Museum, London)

166

NOTES

The principal biography of Elizabeth Inchbald is that by James Boaden, biographer in turn of John Philip Kemble (1825), Mrs. Siddons (1827), Mrs. Jordan (1831) and Elizabeth Inchbald (1833). This is Memoirs of Mrs. Inchbald, published in London by Richard Bentley, and the primary source for any other, later studies of Elizabeth Inchbald, especially the somewhat slight biography, Elizabeth Inchbald and her Circle, by S.R. Littlewood, 1921. Other studies have been far more concerned with specialized critical evaluation than with biography as such, notably William McKee's Elizabeth Inchbald: Novelist (1935), which discusses the Catholic aspects of her two novels, Bruce Robertson Park's Thomas Holcroft and Elizabeth Inchbald: Studies in the 18th Century Drama of Ideas (1952), and Gary Kelly's The English Jacobin Novel 1780-1805 (1976). Specific sources other than Boaden are given in the Notes to each individual chapter.

I. ACTRESS

1. Boaden, Memoirs of Mrs. Inchbald, Vol. I, p.25.
2. The story of Elizabeth Simpson's initial wanderings in London with a growing uncertainty of how to achieve her aim, led later to alternative versions circulating which, no doubt as a result of confused recollections, she appeared to endorse and which her contemporary biographer, Boaden, felt he should at least mention. The alternative story to the one just told shows her arriving in London, going immediately by hackney-coach to the friends she hoped to find in Charing Cross, and, totally put out by their departure, refuse in panic the kindly offer of a night's lodging extended to her by the new tenants. She is represented as having sped away along the streets and taken refuge at the first lodging-house she could find in order to avoid the attentions of a man whose curiosity had been roused by

the evident predicament of this beautiful girl. The landlady, it was alleged, was suspicious enough to threaten to summon a constable. According to this version of her story, Elizabeth finally ended up at the White Swan Inn where, it would seem, the alternate versions of her misadventures converged.

3. According to Boaden, Elizabeth appears to have received at this time letters from a total stranger, a man named Redman, first on 19 April, and twice on 20 April, all of which she appears to have answered promptly, though it would seem she never sent her third response. The nature of this correspondence remains a mystery. For this and the alternative story given in Note 2 above, see Boaden, op.cit. Vol. I, chapter 2.

4. For this, and for the brief quotations above, see Boaden, op.cit., I, pp. 4-7.

5. See Defoe, <u>A Tour Through England and Wales.</u> Edition, Everyman Library (J.M. Dent and Sons), Vol. I, pp. 49, 61.

6. Boaden, op.cit., I, p. 17.

7. Ibid, pp. 14-15.

8. Ibid, p. 18.

9. In other words, the <u>daily</u> consumption of newspapers in Britain today equals approximately the <u>annual</u> consumption in the 1770s. The first <u>daily</u> to be published in England, <u>The Daily Courant</u>, had appeared at the beginning of the century in 1702.

10. Boaden, op.cit., I., p. 27.

11. Catholics and Nonconformists were required by law to be married according to the rites of the Church of England in addition to any ceremony undertaken in their own churches, or at a private house. Compare the double wedding in <u>A Simple Story</u>, edition Oxford University Press paperback, 1977, p. 192, and note.

12. Until the Married Women's Property Act was passed in 1881 in Britain, no married woman could own property outside the control of her husband, though she could benefit under a trust. See Boaden, op.cit., I, p. 53.

13. Boaden, op.cit., I, pp. 48-49.

14. Ibid, p. 68.

15. David Garrick (1716-1779), a pupil of Dr. Johnson when the latter was a schoolmaster in

Lichfield, left with him in 1736 for London, where eventually, in 1741, Garrick began his successful career on the London stage, his management at Drury Lane lasting from 1747 to 1776. Alike a great actor, stage director, and innovator in theatrical presentation, Garrick dominated the English stage during the third quarter of the century.

16. Manchester was second only to London in population in England in the late 18th century, reaching by 1801 some 100,000; in the same period, Liverpool reached 80,000, while Bristol was only some 63,000. For the significance of these various bigger cities theatrically, see Roger Manvell, Sarah Siddons, pp. 39-40.

17. For this, and the quotation above, see Boaden, op.cit., p. 75.

18. In Canterbury, Elizabeth worked with the actor Thomas Holcroft, later to become famous as a dramatist and novelist, and to become her literary adviser.

19. For a fuller account of Tate Wilkinson, see study by Charles Beecher Hogan in The Theatrical Managers in England and America, edited by Joseph W. Donohue, Princeton University Press, 1971. Tate Wilkinson was an enthusiastic admirer of the Inchbalds - 'my well-beloved, my beautiful Mrs. Inchbald ... gained interest in the hearts of the public and the feelings of the manager' he writes in The Wandering Patentee, Vol. I, p. 277, Vol. II, p. 34. Of Inchbald he writes, Vol. I, p. 277: 'I never experienced more ingenuousness, honour, and integrity, nor did I ever know an actor of such universal worth .... He soon grew into great favour, particularly by his performing Justice Credulous, Sir Anthony Absolute, and many comic old gentlemanlike characters ... and he adored his lovely Mrs. Inchbald to a degree of enthusiasm ....'

20. See Sarah Siddons, Roger Manvell, Chapters II and III.

21. According to Boaden, Sarah Siddons worked for Tate Wilkinson in York from Easter to Whitsuntide in 1778. Kemble joined the company in October 1778 and remained until 1781. Elizabeth was a member from 1777-1780.

22. Boaden, op.cit., I, p. 91.

23. Ibid, p. 95.
24. Boaden, <u>Life of Kemble</u>, Vol. I, p. 31. Inchbald's death is told somewhat dramatically by Tate Wilkinson, <u>The Wandering Patentee</u>, Vol. II, p. 56.
25. Boaden, op.cit., Vol. I, pp. 100-101.
26. The benefit system, which lasted until the nineteenth century, brought the popular player, both in London and the provinces, his main opportunity to make money. If his benefit night were 'clear,' the actor drew the total takings, clear of any deduction for the theatre's expenses. A 'shared' benefit meant splitting the night's profits with another player. If star performers consented to act for a fellow-player's benefit, they frequently charged a fee for appearing, mostly below their normal one. Their presence might greatly increase the takings, and the deduction of the star's reduced fee from the takings might still result in a substantial increase in a lesser-known player's benefit.

II. DRAMATIST

The principal source for this chapter continues to be Boaden's <u>Memoirs of Mrs. Inchbald</u>. In consideration of the various plays Elizabeth Inchbald wrote which are the subject of this chapter, readers are referred to the plot synopses and scene quotations in Appendix II.

1. Compare Boaden, op.cit., I, p. 140, and the story that she went to a masquerade in London in male attire for a 'frolic.' Also she had in April 1780 appeared as Hamlet for the benefit of her stepson, George Inchbald. (Boaden, p. 120). Also in Vol. I, chapter 26 of <u>A Simple Story</u>, the heroine dressed herself seemingly in male attire when impersonating the goddess Diana in her guise as a huntress.
2. Boaden, op.cit., Vol. I, p. 107. The word humour is of course used here in its older sense of temperamental tendency.
3. Ibid, pp. 109-13.
4. See Roger Manvell, <u>Sarah Siddons</u>, Chapter III.
5. Boaden, op.cit., I, p. 173.
6. Ibid, p. 174.

7.   Ibid, p. 154.
8.   Ibid, pp. 231-32. John Walcot (1738-1819) was a physician who published satiric verses under the name, Peter Pindar, in 1782, attacking the Royal Academicians. So successful was this publication he followed it up with somewhat scurrilous satire on writers, political ministers, and even the King himself.
9.   Ibid, p. 233.
10. Boaden lists the books she had recorded as reading in successive passages in the Memoirs, for example Vol. I, pp. 170, 179.
11. Boaden, op.cit., Vol. I, p. 159.
12. Ibid, p. 78.
13. Ibid, p. 186.
14. Ibid, p. 187.
15. Ibid, p. 189.
16. Ibid, p. 190. Compare Elizabeth's own, later opinion of such dialogue. See Chapter IV, p. 131.
17. Ibid, p. 209; and the quotation that follows is at p. 222.
18. Rights in the 'copy' of a play did not exist in Shakespeare's time, when the text of a play could only too easily be pirated and printed without the author's knowledge or consent. The only deterrent lay in the State control of all printed works, which from 1556 until 1694 (with minor intermissions) had to receive a license from the Stationer's Company, the company consisting of printers and publishers. Swift is reputed to have drafted the wording of the Act of 1709 'vesting the copies of printed books in the authors or purchasers of such Copies,' with the effect of limiting for a fixed period the rights in all publishing of a work to the author or the person who had bought the copyright from him or her. All titles had still to be registered in Stationers' Hall.
     This situation obtained during the main publishing life of Elizabeth Inchbald, the rights in any work being limited to a period of 14 years only with an extension granted for a further 14 years if the author were still living. During the 19th and 20th centuries considerable extensions to author's rights were to be established. (For a useful summary of this complex matter, see the

Copyright entry in the <u>Oxford Companion to the Theatre</u>, edited by Phyllis Hartnoll, Oxford University Press, 1952, revised edition. Since Colman did not buy the copyright of Elizabeth's play, <u>I'll Tell You What</u>, this left her free to publish the work on her own.

19. Boaden, op.cit., Vol. I, pp. 236-37.
20. She also undertook certain direct translations for Le Texier, Harris' French agent. See Boaden, op.cit., Vol. I, p. 261. Synopses of Elizabeth Inchbald's plays are contained in Appendix II.
21. August Friedrich Ferdinand von Kotzebue (1761-1819) was a German dramatist who also served in various legal and diplomatic posts in the service of Russia, and was also for some years until 1801 director of the German theatre at St. Petersburg. He wrote over 200 plays. He was a strong supporter of the principle of monarchy, and he was fatally stabbed by an angry opponent in 1819. Among his plays was <u>Der Weibliche Jakobinerklub</u> (<u>The Female Jacobin Club</u>, 1793).
22. Her closest women friends at this time were Mrs. Whitfield and the actress, Mrs. Wells of Covent Garden. Even at the age of 35, Elizabeth could be mischievous. Boaden quotes her (op.cit., I, p. 259): 'supped with Mrs. Whitfield. At dark, she and I and her son William walked out. I rapped at doors in New Street and King Street and ran away.'
23. Boaden, op.cit., I, p. 257.
24. Boaden, op.cit., I, p. 258.
25. Her stepson, George Inchbald, the actor, died in 1800.
26. Boaden, op.cit., I, pp. 291 and 307. Another doctor, Dr. Gisborne, was later to become a suitor. See Boaden, op.cit., I, pp. 335 et seq. Things came to something of a head in December 1794. Boaden (op.cit., I, p. 341) records her as writing: 'Dr. Gisborne drank tea here, and staid very late: he talked seriously of <u>marrying</u> - but not ME.' The next day she wrote, 'Happy at Dr. Gisborne's behaviour, notwithstanding what he said.' She set about 'contriving brave punishments,' for him. But they were soon on good terms again. Boaden gives many of his letters to

172

Elizabeth which she obviously kept.

27. Boaden, op.cit., I, p. 310.
28. Boaden, op.cit., I, p. 311.
29. Boaden analyzes the principal changes made in
    Lovers' Vows, op.cit., II, p. 21, and
    mentions her many adjustments in The Wise Man
    of the East after its initial indifferent
    reception in November 1799. See Boaden,
    op.cit., II, p. 27.
30. Boaden, op.cit., II, pp. 24-26.
31. Boaden, op.cit., II, pp. 26-27.
32. In 1801 Godwin was to marry (unhappily) Mary
    Jane Clairmont, mother of Jane (Claire)
    Clairmont, later to become notorious as Lord
    Byron's mistress.
33. Boaden, op.cit., II, p. 328.
34. Boaden (Memoirs, II, p. 4) quotes Elizabeth
    herself on this point in relation to Wives as
    They Were. 'She had written it with extreme
    care as to the brilliancy and point of the
    dialogue; and as to some improbabilities in
    the structure and progress of the fable,
    though she had felt them all, she yet thought
    them within the modern limits of critical
    indulgence. Indeed, she saw, for the most
    part of her experience, that the manner was
    nearly everything; and if you could but hit
    upon the right mode, the objectionable in the
    abstract would pass upon the stage as it does
    in real life.'
35. See John Genest, Some Account of the English
    Stage - 1660 to 1830, Vols. VI and VII under
    appropriate years.
36. See Gary Kelly, The English Jacobin Novel, p.
    65.
37. See Jane Austen, Mansfield Park, Chapters
    XIV, XV.
38. See Kelly, op.cit., p. 94 et seq.
39. Warren Hastings (1732-1818), English colonial
    administrator attached to the East India
    Company, serving in Calcutta, Madras and
    Bengal, became the first Governor-General of
    India in 1773, with divergent (and sometimes
    contradictory) responsibilities, both
    political and commercial. Although he
    favored employing Indians where possible, he
    ruled autocratically and many of his agents
    were seriously corrupt. Bribery was
    rampant. Members of his own Council turned
    against him and many difficulties led to his

resignation in 1785. He was impeached before the House of Lords, the hearings lasting ten years, his successive accusers being Charles James Fox, Edmund Burke and Richard Brinsley Sheridan. His trial, the longest political trial in British history, ended with his acquittal in 1795, and official rehabilitation in 1813. The trial was perhaps more of an attack on the system than the man himself.

40. See Kelly, op.cit., p. 96, and Boaden, Memoirs, I, p. 294.
41. See C. Kegan Paul, William Godwin: his Friends and Contemporaries, Vol. I, p. 141. For Hardinge's letter see Boaden, Memoirs, Vol. I, p. 328.
42. See Allardyce Nicoll, A History of English Drama 1660-1900, Vol. III, Late Eighteenth Century Drama 1750-1800, pp. 147 et seq.
43. Bruce Robertson Park, Thomas Holcroft and Elizabeth Inchbald: Studies in the Eighteenth Century Drama of Ideas. Columbia University Ph.D. Thesis, 1952.

III. NOVELIST

1. This essay appears in Virginia Woolf's Granite and Rainbow (Hogarth Press, 1958).
2. The title of Jane Austen's first novel, Sense and Sensibility (1811) echoes Elizabeth's Nature and Art.
3. Aphra Behn (1640-89), dramatist and story writer, published a century before Elizabeth's work, Oroonoko (c. 1678), later dramatized by Southerne. Oroonoko embodied the concept of the 'noble savage' in the character of a slave of royal birth who is cruelly treated by his British masters in the West Indies, and attempts a double suicide along with his equally noble love.
4. See Walter Allen, The English Novel (Penguin Books), p. 14.
5. There are some exceptions to this – Shakespeare's realistic prose dialogue in Henry IV Parts i and ii, and certain of Jonson's plays.
6. Allen, op.cit., p. 49.
7. In a notable preface to Joseph Andrews, Fielding defines his approach to the ridiculous, the exposure in comic terms of

vanity and hypocrisy, just as Ben Jonson had done before him in drama.

8. It is worth noting Diderot's definition of sensibility, quoted by Allardyce Nicoll in History of English Drama 1660-1900, Vol. III, Late Eighteenth Century Drama, p. 147: '... la sensibilité, selon la seule acception qu'on ait donnée jusqu'à présent à ce terme, est ... cette disposition .... qui incline à compatir, à frissonner, à admirer, à craindre, à se troubler, à pleurer, à s'évanouir, à sécourir.'

9. Allen, op.cit., p. 8.

10. See Introduction by J.M.S. Tompkins to the Oxford University Press edition of A Simple Story (1967), p. xi.

11. See Tompkins, Introduction op.cit., and Note on Text, p. xvii et seq. For the reference to Godwin's diary, see C. Kegan Paul, William Godwin and his Friends and Contemporaries, Vol. I, p. 66.

12. Elizabeth herself had undergone the double marriage ceremony, as required by law, being married in her sister's house on 9 June 1772 by a Catholic priest, and on 10 June in a Protestant church. One of the reasons for this law was to prevent clandestine marriages by Catholics and Nonconformists.

13. A Simple Story in its original form was very short by the standards set by most novels of the period - only some 60,000 words. Contrast Fanny Burney's Evelina (150,000). Goldsmith's Vicar of Wakefield, however, was only some 75,000 words, and Maria Edgeworth's Castle Rackrent was only some 30,000. The normal length of Jane Austen's novels was to be in the area of 150,000 words.

14. One wonders whether Elizabeth inserted the story of Elmwood's rejection of his nephew in order to anticipate his parallel rejection of Matilda in Part Two. The story of the nephew is somewhat intrusive, but he is of course to become a protagonist in Part Two.

15. Some 800 people died in the week-long riots, which turned into a bloody demonstration. The riots are described by Dickens in Barnaby Rudge.

16. Walter Allen in The English Novel singles out Mrs. Charlotte Smith's The Old Manor House (1793) for some praise, but again this novel

appeared after the first edition of <u>A Simple Story</u>.

17. See Chapter IV, p. 17.
18. All quotations from <u>A Simple Story</u> are taken from the Oxford University Press paperback edition of 1977. For the description of Dorriforth, see page 8.
19. <u>A Simple Story</u>, p. 223.
20. Op.cit., p. 15.
21. Op.cit., p. 9.
22. Op.cit., pp. 39-40.
23. Op.cit., pp. 28-30.
24. Op.cit., pp. 72-73.
25. Op.cit., p. 82.
26. Op.cit., pp. 148-49.
27. Op.cit., pp. 35-36.
28. Op.cit., pp. 204-05.
29. Op.cit., pp. 273-74.
30. Kelly, <u>The English Jacobin Novel</u>, p. 66.
31. McKee, <u>Elizabeth Inchbald, Novelist</u>, p. 75.
32. Kelly, op.cit. The quotations in this paragraph are at pages 71-79.
33. For these two quotations, see William Hazlitt, <u>Complete Works</u>, Dent 1930-34, Vol. XVII, p. 251, and Vol. XII, p. 303.
34. Joughin, <u>The Life and Work of Elizabeth Inchbald</u>, p. 309.
35. <u>A Simple Story</u>, p. 221.
36. The facts given in this section are derived mainly from Ford K. Brown's <u>The Life of William Godwin</u> (London, J.M. Dent, 1926) and C. Kegan Paul's <u>William Godwin: his Friends and Contemporaries</u> (New York, AMS Press, 1970; reprinted from the 1876 edition in two volumes). For Godwin's first contact with Elizabeth, see Brown, p. 42.
37. This proposal seems slightly odd; Godwin disapproved of marriage on principle, while Elizabeth was determined to remain the independent friend of the men she favored, and no man's wife or mistress.
38. Paul, op.cit., Vol. I, p. 74.
39. Paul, op.cit., Vol. I, pp. 138-39.
40. Paul, op.cit., Vol. I, p. 139.
41. Paul, op.cit., Vol. I, p. 140. See chap. II above p. 20.
42. Details concerning Mary Wollstonecraft are taken from Emily W. Sunstein's <u>A Different Face: Life of Mary Wollstonecraft</u> (New York, Harper and Row, 1975) and Ralph M. Wardle,

<u>Collected Letters of Mary Wollstonecraft</u>
(Cornell University Press, 1979). According
to a letter Amelia Alderson wrote in the
summer of 1795, Godwin and Holcroft were the
center of female attention: 'Mrs. Inchbald
says, the report of the world is, that Mr.
Holcroft is in love with her, <u>she</u> with Mr.
Godwin, Mr. Godwin with <u>me</u>, and I <u>am</u> in love
with Mr. Holcroft! A pretty story indeed.'
(See Marshall, <u>William Godwin</u>, p. 174.)

43.   See Sunstein, op.cit., p. 326.
44.   <u>Memoirs of Mary Wollstonecraft</u>, by William
      Godwin, edition London, Constable and Co.,
      1928, p. 106.
45.   Paul, op.cit., Vol. I, p. 240.
46.   Brown, op.cit., p. 120.
47.   Brown, op.cit., p. 121.
48.   Brown, op.cit., p. 129.
49.   Paul, op.cit., Vol. I, p. 276.
50.   Paul, op.cit., Vol. I, p. 277.
51.   Paul, op.cit., Vol. I, p. 277.
52.   Paul, op.cit., Vol. I, p. 278.
53.   Boaden, op.cit., Vol. II, p. 14.
54.   Paul, op.cit., Vol. I, p. 279.
55.   Paul, op.cit., Vol. I, p. 279.   See also
      Boaden, op.cit., Vol. II, p. 30.
56.   See Brown, op.cit., p. 134.
57.   Boaden, op.cit., Vol. II, p. 29.
58.   Paul, op.cit., Vol. I, p. 350.
59.   See McKee, <u>Elizabeth Inchbald, Novelist</u>, p.
      16.
60.   McKee, op.cit., p. 18.
61.   The principal Jacobin-influenced novels were
      Holcroft's <u>Alwyn</u> (1780) and <u>Anna St. Ives</u>
      (1792), Bage's <u>Man as He Is</u> (1792), Godwin's
      <u>Caleb Williams</u>, or <u>Things as They Are</u> (1794),
      Holcroft's <u>Hugh Trevor</u> (1794-7), Elizabeth
      Inchbald's <u>Nature and Art</u> (1796), Bage's
      <u>Hermsprong</u> (1796), Godwin's <u>St. Leon</u> (1799),
      <u>Fleetwood</u>   (1805),   <u>Mandeville</u>   (1817),
      <u>Cloudesley</u> (1830) and <u>Deloraine</u> (1833).
62.   William Hazlitt, Complete Works, J.M. Dent
      1930-34. Vol. VI, p. 123.
63.   Compare Voltaire's <u>Candide</u>, and Bage's
      <u>Hermsprong</u>, in which the young hero is reared
      among North American Indians.
64.   It would seem in some earlier editions the
      name of this character was Hannah, and that
      Elizabeth subsequently changed this to
      Agnes. Agnes's fate in London was in some

measure similar to that of Elizabeth's sister, Dolly, who died in 1794.

65. In _Emile_ (1762) Rousseau contends that children should be regarded as such and brought up 'naturally' to develop into men and women. Emile is a fictitious private pupil who is reared humanely, without excessive indulgence or severity, and without the false, unnatural institutionalizing which conditions children to fit into an unnatural civilization in what Rousseau calls the 'ridiculous establishments called colleges.' When the child is ready to reason at the stage of adolescence and understand the nature of ideas, then ideas can be introduced; up to that time, education should allow the child to respond naturally to his or her actual needs, exercising and developing the body and the senses, combining work with play, punishment springing from his or her own actions. Friendship should precede actual love and sex, which should come as late in youth as possible; corruption in sex derives from the corruption of society. Emile studies the state of society and the nature of government by taking a 'grand tour' of the most degenerate societies of Europe to the least degenerate. While still young he meets and falls in love with Sophie, an ideal girl ideally raised. They marry; he becomes her tutor, but not immediately. Rousseau maintains it is bad for a still-growing girl to conceive a child.

66/67. Quotations from _Nature and Art_ are taken from the edition of 1886 published in Cassell of London's National Library. These quotations come at pages 28-29 and 33.

68. _Nature and Art_, op.cit., p. 69.
69. _Nature and Art_, op.cit., p. 18.
70. _Nature and Art_, op.cit., p. 23.
71. _Nature and Art_, op.cit., pp. 47, 49.
72. _Nature and Art_, op.cit., p. 36.
73. _Nature and Art_, op.cit., p. 57.
74. _Nature and Art_, op.cit., p. 43.
75. _Nature and Art_, op.cit., p. 54.
76. _Nature and Art_, op.cit., p. 78

IV.   CRITIC, AND HISTORIAN OF
        THE BRITISH THEATRE

The introductory comments written by Elizabeth
Inchbald for the 25-volume anthology of plays, The
British Theatre (1808) form the primary source for
this chapter. Since the five plays making up each
volume with their introductions are page-numbered
individually, the many comments quoted in this
chapter can only be referred to by indicating the
number of the volume in which each play appears.
They are listed below in alphabetic order of title;
dates are given for plays from the Restoration
period to the early 19th century:

All in the Wrong (Murphy, 1761), Vol. XV
Antony and Cleopatra (Shakespeare), Vol. IV
As You Like It (Shakespeare), Vol. III
The Beaux' Stratagem (Farquhar, 1707), Vol. VIII
The Beggar's Opera (Gay, 1728), Vol. XII
The Belles' Stratagem (Mrs. Cowley, 1780), Vol. XIX
A Bold Stroke for a Wife (Mrs. Centlivre, 1718),
        Vol. XI
The Brothers (Cumberland, 1769), Vol. XVIII
Cato (Addison, 1713), Vol. VIII
The Conscious Lovers (Steele, 1722), Vol. XII
The Country Girl (Garrick, 1766), Vol. XVI
Cymbeline (Shakespeare), Vol. IV
De Monfort (Joanna Baillie, 1798), Vol. XXIV
The Dramatist (Reynolds, 1789), Vol. XX
The Duenna (Sheridan, 1775), Vol. XIX
George Barnwell (The London Merchant, Lillo, 1731),
        Vol. XI
Henry IV, Part I (Shakespeare), Vol. II
Henry V (Shakespeare), Vol. II
Henry VIII (Shakespeare), Vol. III
Inkle and Yarico (Colman the Younger, 1796),
        Vol. XX
The Iron Chest (Colman the Younger, 1796), Vol. XXI
Isabella, or the Fatal Marriage (Southerne, 1694),
        Vol. VII
The Jew (Cumberland, 1794), Vol. XVIII
John Bull (Colman the Younger, 1803), Vol. XXI
King John (Shakespeare), Vol. I
King Lear (Shakespeare), Vol. IV
The London Merchant (Barnwell, Lillo, 1731), Vol. XI
Macbeth (Shakespeare), Vol. IV
Measure for Measure (Shakespeare), Vol. III
The Mountaineers (Colman the Younger, 1793),
        Vol. XXI

The Mourning Bride (Congreve, 1697), Vol. VIII
Oroonoko (Southerne, 1695), Vol. VII
The Revenge (Young, 1721), Vol. XII
Richard III (Shakespeare), Vol. I
The Rival Queens (Lee, 1677), Vol. VI
The Rivals (Sheridan, 1775), Vol. XIX
The Road to Ruin (Holcroft, 1792), Vol. XXIV
Romeo and Juliet (Shakespeare), Vol. I
She Stoops to Conquer (Goldsmith, 1773), Vol. XVII
She Wou'd and She Wou'd Not (Cibber, 1702), Vol. IX
Wheel of Fortune (Cumberland, 1795), Vol. XVIII

Notes for this chapter indicated by superior
figures follow:

1. See The British Theatre, Vol. XXI.
2. The prefaces were, of course, intended for
    the general reader, not the scholar, or the
    literary or dramatic critic.
3. For this and the quotations following, see
    Allardyce Nicoll, A History of English Drama
    1660 to 1900, Vol. III, pp. 5, 10, 15-16.
4. George Lillo's play, Fatal Curiosity (or,
    Guilt its own Punishment, 1736, but presented
    by Elizabeth Inchbald as altered by Colman,
    1783), is described by Allardyce Nicoll as an
    example of 'sentimentalized bourgeois
    drama.' It is a domestic tragedy of three
    acts written in verse. Set in Penryn, near
    Falmouth in Cornwall, and based on what is
    alleged to have been a real-life incident, it
    involves an elderly couple, Wilmot and his
    wife Agnes, who live on in penury, believing
    that their son, who has in the past gone away
    to India, is now dead. But Young Wilmot
    returns. He chooses to visit his parents in
    disguise, taking with him a casket of
    jewels. The sight of this wealth destroys
    their consciences, and, like Macbeth and Lady
    Macbeth, they are driven by want to murder
    their guest, Agnes urging her husband to
    commit the crime. When they realize the
    truth, that it is indeed their own son that
    they have murdered, Old Wilmot turns on his
    wife and kills her, and then commits
    suicide. Colman modified the violence in the
    play, toning down the dialogue.
5. It should not be overlooked that Elizabeth
    Inchbald was herself the writer of farces as
    well as comedies. She included Child of

180

Nature, The Wedding Day, and The Midnight
Hour in her self-selected Collection of
Farces and other Afterpieces collected into
seven volumes in 1809.
6. See for example, M.W. Black and M.A. Shaaber,
Shakespeare's Seventeenth Century Editors
1632-1685, New York, MLA, 1937; Montagu
Summers (ed.), Shakespeare Adaptations: The
Tempest, The Mock Tempest, King Lear, New
York, Haskell House, 1966; Davenant's Macbeth
from the Yale Manuscript, edited by
Christopher Spencer, New Haven, Yale
University Press, 1961; and Nahum Tate, The
History of King Lear, edited by James Black,
Lincoln, University of Nebraska Press, 1975.

V. THE LAST YEARS

1. She was buried in Kensington churchyard. The
inscription, given by Boaden, op.cit., II, p.
279, reads: 'Sacred to the Memory of
Elizabeth Inchbald, Whose Writings will be
cherished While Truth, Simplicity, and
Feeling Command public Admiration; And whose
retired and exemplary Life Closed, as it
existed, In Acts of Charity and Benevolence.
She died 1 August 1821, Aged 63 Years.' The
wording was composed by John Taylor.
2. Boaden, op.cit., Vol. II, p. 55; the
quotations following at p. 58, and p. 91.
3. Boaden, op.cit., Vol. II, p. 162.
4. Boaden, op.cit., Vol. II, p. 216.
5. Boaden, op.cit., gives details of her
holdings Vol. II, pp. 229 and 257. For her
will and its many small bequests, see p. 284.
6. The Artist, 13 June 1807. Reprinted by
William McKee in Elizabeth Inchbald as an
Appendix, p. 153.
7. Boaden, op.cit., Vol. II, p. 57.
8. Boaden, op.cit., Vol. II, p. 63.
9. Boaden, op.cit., Vol. II, p. 75.
10. Taylor, Records of my Life, p. 408.
11. Its table of Contents did, however, survive,
and is given by Boaden, op.cit., Vol. II, p.
232.
12. Boaden, op.cit., Vol. II, p. 14.
13. Boaden, op.cit., Vol. II, p. 31.
14. See Boaden, op.cit., Vol. II, p. 123, for
examples.
15. Boaden, op.cit., Vol. II, p. 282.

16. Boaden, op.cit., Vol. II, p. 40.
17. Boaden, op.cit., Vol. II, p. 43; original in Folger Shakespeare Library.
18. For Master Betty's career, see the biography by Giles Playfair. Sarah Siddons was equally caustic in her comments on this phenomenal child actor who stole audiences away from the adult star players. See Manvell, <u>Sarah Siddons</u>, p. 284. The same thing happened in Shakespeare's time; see, for example, Rosencrantz's comment in <u>Hamlet</u>, Act. II, ii. on the popularity of the boy players.
19. Boaden, op.cit., Vol. II, p. 78.
20. Boaden, op.cit., Vol. II, p. 177.
21. Boaden, op.cit., Vol. II, p. 82.
22. Boaden, op.cit., Vol. II, p. 221.
23. Boaden, op.cit., Vol. II, p. 222.
24. Taylor, op.cit., p. 397.
25. Taylor, op.cit., p. 405.
26. Taylor, op.cit., p. 408. Taylor also tells an amusing story of an attempt by Harris of Covent Garden to persuade Elizabeth to grant him the kind of favors he enjoyed with other actresses: 'At his desire, Mrs. Inchbald attended him one morning at his house at Knightsbridge, to consult on one of her plays which was soon to be represented. When the consultation was ended, Mr. Harris, who was a handsome man, and found so little difficulty among the theatrical sisterhood under his government, thought that he might be equally successful in an attack on Mrs. Inchbald, but, instead of regular approaches, he attempted to take the fort by storm, and Mrs. Inchbald found no resource but in seizing him by his hair, which she pulled with such violence, that she forced him to desist. She then rushed out of the house, and proceeded in haste, and under great agitation, to the green-room of the theatre, where the company were then rehearsing. She entered the room with so wild an air, and with such evident emotion, that all present were alarmed. She hastily related what had happened as far as her impediment would permit her, and concluded with the following exclamation: 'Oh! if he had wo-wo-worn a wig, I had been ru-ruined.' (p. 399).
27. Preserved in the Enthoven Collection, Victoria and Albert Museum, London. Taylor,

according to himself, <u>Records</u>, p. 402, composed the doggerel verses of the Rhyming Butler in <u>Lovers' Vows</u>, and Elizabeth insisted that he receive from her a fee for this.

28. Boaden, op.cit., Vol. II, pp. 152-155.
29. Boaden, op.cit., Vol. II, p. 176.
30. Mme. de Staël (1766-1817), daughter of Jacques Necker, French Minister of Finance at the period of the Revolution, was a novelist and essayist and brought up in literary circles in Paris. She herself established a liberal, pre-Revolutionary salon in the capital, but left France at the time of the Revolution and settled in Switzerland, returning only to be banished by her enemy, Napoleon, following the publication of her novel, <u>Delphine</u> (1802). She had been married to the Baron de Staël, Swedish ambassador to France, but they separated. She resettled in Paris only after the fall of Napoleon. Her work included <u>Lettres sur Jean-Jacques Rousseau</u> (1789), <u>Corinne</u> (1807), <u>Réflexions sur le Suicide</u> (1813), the year she met Elizabeth. Her <u>Considerations sur la Révolution française</u> appeared in 1818. Her study of German literature banned in France by Napoleon appeared in England in 1813.
31. Boaden, op.cit., Vol. II, p. 190.
32. Rogers, <u>Table Talk</u>, p. 201.
33. Boaden, op.cit., Vol. II, p. 126.
34. Boaden, op.cit., Vol. II, pp. 171 and 183.
35. Boaden, op.cit., Vol. I, p. 175.
36. John Genest (1764-1839) created his celebrated and very reliable book of reference, <u>Some Account of the English Stage from the Restoration in 1660 to 1830</u>, published in 1832. His description of Elizabeth appears in Vol. VII, p. 669.

Theatre-Royal, Covent-Garden.

This present TUESDAY, OCTOBER 3, 1780,

A PLAY, called

PHILASTER.

Philaster by Mr. LEWIS,

(Being his First Appearance in that Character.)

King by Mr. L'ESTRANGE,

Pharamond by Mr. WHITFIELD,

Thrafaline, Mr. THOMPSON, Cleremont, Mr. ROBSON,

Woodman, Mr. BOOTH, Capt. of the Mob, Mr. FEARON,

Dion by Mr. HULL,

Arethufa by Mrs. MATTOCKS,

Megra by Mifs AMBROSSE,

Lady by Mrs. POUSSIN, Galatea by Mifs STEWART,

And Bellario by Mrs. INCHBALD,

(Being her First Appearance in LONDON.)

End of Act II. The SHEPHERD'S WEDDING, by Mr. HARRIS & Mifs MATTHEWS.

End of Act III. The HUMOURS of LEIXLIP,

By Mr. ALDRIDGE, Mr. LANGRISH, and Mifs BESFORD.

Playbill for Philaster
at Theatre Royal Covent Garden (1780),
with Elizabeth Inchbald as Bellario.
(Enthoven Collection,
Vctoria and Albert Museum, (London)

APPENDIX ONE

COLLECTIONS OF ELIZABETH INCHBALD'S LETTERS,

MEMORANDA AND ITEMS OF HER PERSONAL ARCHIVE

HELD AT THE BRITISH MUSEUM AND

THE FOLGER SHAKESPEARE LIBRARY

The British Museum in London in its Manuscript Department (46611 ff 260-263; 27 925 f 24, 28 558 f83) holds part, if not all of the manuscript sources placed at the disposal of Boaden by Elizabeth Inchbald's literary executor, Mrs. Frances Phillips, 'for the purpose of writing and preparing a life of the late Elizabeth Inchbald,' whom Mrs. Phillips terms 'the cleverest, self-educated woman that lived.' This source material included sixty pocketbooks, three memorandum books, twenty-four letters from the Edgeworth family, over a hundred letters from George Colman, Sarah Siddons, the Kembles and others, business letters relating to her engagements as an actress, benefit performance accounts from Covent Garden and the Haymarket Theatres, as well as letters to and from her relatives.

The Folger Shakespeare Library has a considerable collection of interesting material relating to Elizabeth Inchbald. This material includes, in addition to letters and private notes about herself, a number of her 'pocketbooks' (or day-by-day engagement diaries), and records of receipts for her plays on four nights at the Haymarket Theatre, 1784-86. There is also a copy of her Will (1821), and a collection of quotations from authors she read, and some casual comments on actors made in or around 1801. A quotation of interest is one from Johnson: 'A man who keeps his money has in reality more use from it than he can have from spending it.'

Elizabeth Inchbald began to keep a diary in

185

1770, and it would seem maintained it until 1820, using each year a standard published volume called The Ladies Own Memorandum Book. The volumes surviving at the Library are for the years 1776, 1780, 1781, 1783, 1788, 1807, 1808, 1814, and 1820. One of the notes about herself (undated, but belonging to the period when she was under the medical care of Dr. Warren) survives together with a follow-up note written some years later, and also undated. It is headed, Comforts, and continues, with some words illegible indicated thus [ ]:

I have been cured of my dizziness - so was my mother
I lost the low spirits I had in Scotland which were dreadful [   ] recovered Low Spirits
I have lost the difficulty of sighing or breathing which so long afflicted me
Got rid of my fainting sensations too
[   ] face numb and nervous
How many have even strokes and recover
Dr. Warren assures me it is not so

The second note follows:

Many years since the above was written. I add I have lost that numbness or stiffness in my face. Small convulsions I had also in my face and now I have nearly wholly lost them.

Flakes of fire from my eyes are too gone or proved to be only the consequence of fright in waking from dreams.

The sensation at my heart at times so alarming is for years without returning, or returning in the slightest manner. The spasmodic affection of my head returns but seldom and is of but slight inconvenience.

The nervous sensation I had when a child and once in my youth of seeing everything larger I never had since I married. Dimness of sight and flashing of the eyes have proved but temporary.

The collection of letters includes notes addressed to many people of note, including Sheridan, Sarah Siddons, Harris (the Manager of

186

Covent Garden Theatre), and Tate Wilkinson. A selection of these is given below:

To Mr. James Northcote (Friday 30 January; no year):

> To prevent a similar mortification to that I received yesterday evening by being unable to admit you, I give you this information - I am so situated in this house I can never receive a visitor but at certain hours - from half past two to half past four I sit in state - the remainder of the day has so much the reverse of dignity that retirement to concealment is requisite for my friends' convenience as much as for my own.

To R.B. Sheridan (5 May 1792):

> There are few things that could give me so much pain as the being guilty of the impertinence of troubling you with a letter - but the necessities of any author once more compel me. Mr. Kemble many weeks ago purchased a farce of me in your name, at the same time assuring me it should be performed immediately - but as I have reason to apprehend, from the near approach of the close of the Theatre, that it cannot be brought out this season. I take the liberty to acquaint you that if either Mr. Kemble in delivering your message, or I in comprehending of it, have made the least mistake in respect to your meaning, and you will be so obliging as to let me know it, I shall instantly relinquish the claim which at present I hope I have on the Theatre, and ask for nothing more than to receive back my manuscript; which (as I have not another copy, and this is the only probable time for Colman to receive it) is of very material consequence to me. In the most earnest manner I therefore entreat, that if you keep the piece any time longer than the following week, you will do me the very great service to give me an order upon your treasurer for two hundred pounds - for which I shall ever

remain, Sir, Your most <u>obliged</u> and most
humble servant, E. Inchbald.

To Tate Wilkinson (1780, otherwise undated):

You surely forget that I am articled and
will stay with you just as long as I
please, therefore don't effront me or
perhaps out of spite I may stay with you
all the Winter - however I believe I
shall go away on the 8th, and as you
think the Countess of Salisbury of such
material consequence get through it as
best I can rather than keep money from
the House - I have nothing to say
against Mrs. Smith, she is a Woman I
admire very much - I will make this
observation, that had she been compelled
to play second parts in the tragedys
with me, as I have in the comedys with
her, she might have been thought as
little of as I am at present - so far
does the success of an actor depend on
the partiality of a Manager. Under you
I never could be a favorite anywhere.

Give me leave to acknowledge the
many favours and <u>great civilities</u> I have
received both from you and Mrs.
Wilkinson as Mrs. Inchbald - but as an
actress?-

Mrs. Smith you know is not the
first by a Dozen that you have preferred
to me - I have been three years with you
at an inferior salary which before I
never received. I have laboured (except
for the three months chance gave the
Management to another) through the most
disadvantageous tho: consequential fast
- I have lost my Beauty and what is
worse my Health by an uncommon attention
to my Business - and with a Prudence
that almost amounted to Penury during
the whole time, (had you it in your
power to discharge me now and pay me no
more salary) I could not leave the
company without parting with some few
properties I brought with me to it -
This is all true. - You assure me there

188

is not a creature in town that regrets my going away - I believe you find the greatest satisfaction in all the above reflection for [to] sum them up, and I think I may 'Boldly venture to a World Unknown.' Your very humble servant, E. Inchbald.

This letter, like the one that follows, was written during the period she was in secret negotiation with Harris of Covent Garden to move to London. The following undated letter was written from Standingfield; and was in response to one she had received from Wilkinson, writing from Sheffield:

Your letter arrived safe and oh it is as well it did, for I am sure had it fallen into any hand but my own, blasted for ever must have been my fair name - I have not done blushing at the contents yet - however as it has contributed to the Beauty of my complexion, you may send me another when it suits you - but pray let me get to London first, nor stain the purity of this sweet Retreat - I am so very happy in my retirement I have not a Wish to come even to you but next summer I shall hope you may again flatter me with an invitation - since I arrived here Mr. Niell has invited me to a Theatre Royal at Windsor - but if I had wanted an engagement I should not have chosen to have embarked on such a scheme - they offer a fine salary ....

ELIZABETH INCHBALD'S PLAYS

Brief Synopses, with
Production and Bibliographical
Dating

Play	First Produced	First Published
A MOGUL TALE	1784	1788

Presented at the Little Theatre, Haymarket. A farcical comedy in two acts. Three people flying in a balloon from London (a Doctor; a cobbler and his wife) land by accident near the Seraglio on the estate of a great Mogul. To save themselves, the Doctor poses as an Ambassador, while the cobbler pretends to be the Pope and his wife, a renegade nun. The Mogul and his lively wives (one of them played by Elizabeth Inchbald) have fun at these visitors' expense; their absurd impostures are soon discovered, and after dire threats are offered them they are eventually released and allowed to fly away.

According to Boaden (Memoirs, Vol. I, p. 158), this farce was originally titled A Peep into a Planet, and written 1781-82, and submitted to Colman under the name of Mrs. Woodley. After much revision had been undertaken, Colman eventually accepted it on 7 March 1784. Balloon ascents became the cause of much popular excitement initially in France during the 1780s. The Montgolfiers' experiments with full-scale balloons began in 1783 and were followed in the same year by Rozier's pioneer ascent by man in a captive balloon. Subsequently, Charles traveled 43 km. suspended by a balloon filled with hydrogen. The first ascent in Britain was made by James Tytler in 1784, the year of the play, and the English Channel was first crossed by balloon in the same year.

I'LL TELL YOU WHAT	1785	1786

Presented at the Little Theatre, Haymarket.

a comedy of intrigue in five acts. Euston and his brother Anthony are returned from the West Indies after long absence only to find their nephew, Sir George Euston, divorced from his wife, Lady Harriet, who has since married her lover, the libertine Major Cyprus, while Sir George has taken a new wife. Cyprus is now intent on seducing this second Lady Euston, while Euston himself remains pathologically jealous of Lady Harriet. Meantime, the two elderly uncles become involved in a secondary, unrelated intrigue. Lady Harriet manages to lure her former husband into a compromising situation in which her second, unfaithful husband discovers him, exactly as he had once been discovered by Sir George.

APPEARANCE IS AGAINST THEM 1785   1785

A comedy in two acts presented at Covent Garden. This centers round the whereabouts of an oriental shawl given to Lady Mary by Warmsley, her betrothed, but stolen by her friend, Miss Angle, to use as a means to attract the libertine Lord Lighthead. She alleges he had sent it to her as a present. Lighthead however is compromised in the eyes of his mistress, Miss Audley, when the amorous Lady Loveall is discovered concealed in his bedroom. Confusion is worse confounded when Warmsley, visiting Lighthead, finds himself in the same room as Lady Loveall, a room where Miss Audley is also concealed; the much-sought shawl arrives, sent by Miss Angle, and Lady Mary, anxious to retrieve her fiancé's valued present, is horrified to find it in the possession of Lady Loveall. Miss Angle's misdeeds are duly exposed, and Warmsley (who had proved not unwilling to forego matrimony) is reconciled to his betrothed.

THE WIDOW'S VOW 1786   1786

Presented at the Little Theatre, Haymarket. A comedy in two acts adapted from Patrat's L'Heureuse Erreur, set in Spain. The Countess lives in seclusion, having vowed to avoid the very sight of men (except that of her uncle Antonio, who resides with her) after enduring a disastrous first marriage. Her neighbor, Donna Isabella, has a young brother, a marquis, who is intent on getting

somehow into the Countess's presence, so Isabella
initiates a plan to visit the Countess disguised
(for a joke between them) as a man. The Countess
agrees, but Isabella sends her brother in her
place, accompanied by a manservant disguised, in
his turn, as a maid. This comedy of disguises and
misunderstandings, played out with the joyous help
of the protagonists' various servants, leads to the
Countess becoming attracted by the Marquis (who of
course she initially believes to be Isabella), and
in the end she consents, to her uncle's delight, to
risk matrimony again when the deception is finally
revealed to her.

SUCH THINGS ARE   1787   1788

     Presented at Covent Garden, this five-act
play is one of Elizabeth Inchbald's most effective
original plays, a mixture of comic satire, drama of
sentiment, and work suggesting prison reform. Its
exotic setting is the island of Sumatra in the East
Indies, where a tyrannical Sultan holds sway but
where English residents and visitors are a
recognized part of the social scene. Sir Luke and
Lady Tremor are satirized as a socially pretentious
couple friendly with Lord Flint, the Sultan's
hard-faced agent, and the Hon. Mr. Twineall is a
confidence trickster who apes the latest fads and
fashions of London society. However, the Sultan
himself turns out to be an imposter who has seized
power and become a tyrant lamenting a long-lost
love, Arabella. The good character in the play is
a Mr. Haswell identified with prison reform and
modeled (as Elizabeth Inchbald pointed out) on a
real-life character, John Howard. Several scenes
show Haswell visiting the Sultan's dungeons; among
the prisoners is a woman, who turns out to be
Arabella. The Sultan, his conscience fully moved,
admits that he is really a Christian; reunited with
Arabella, his nature is changed and he adopts the
kindly Haswell as his prime adviser.

THE MIDNIGHT HOUR   1787   1787

     This short three-act comedy, presented at
Covent Garden, freely translated from the French
and the following on an earlier, published
translation of a play by M. Dumaniant called Guerre

Play	First Produced	First Published

Ouverte, ou Ruse Contre Ruse, is set in Spain, and concerns the intrigues of a young marquis and his conniving servant, Sebastian, to win the hand of Julia, niece of a wealthy general who is determined to marry her to a rich merchant whom neither of them have ever seen, and who never appears as an on-stage character in the play. Their many ruses, unsuccessful at first, to remove the only too willing Julia from her uncle's clutches make up the action of the play.

ALL ON A SUMMER'S DAY   1787   Not published

A comedy in five acts, presented at Covent Garden Theatre; the manuscript is preserved in the Larpent Collection, Huntington Library. The elderly Sir William Carrol lives in the country with his youthful and amusingly contrary wife, Lady Carrol and Sir William's sister, Mrs. Goodly, who acts as her confidante. She admits she does not love her husband and is perversely upset that his friend, the lecherous Wildlove seduces the maidservants and pays her no attention.

A near neighbor, Lady Henrietta, reputedly suffering from a 'nervous disorder' is seen much in the company of another neighbor, Chrysostom, an avowed bachelor. The center of action shifts to Lady Henrietta's dressingroom; successively Wildlove, Chrysostom, Lady Carrol and Sir William arrive either to gossip or attempt love-making. Sir William brings news of new arrivals from India - an old friend Governor Moreton, his daughter, Louisa, her fiancé, Lord Henley. Mrs. Goodly had in the past acted for a period as guardian to Louisa, who is deeply disturbed to learn of Wildlove's presence, as is Lady Carrol in her turn, since at a recent ball she had flirted with Lord Henley and led him to believe Sir William was her father. A further character, the myopic Sir Ralph Mooneye, complicates Lady Carrol's life, leading to a network of absurd impersonations, Lady Carrol pretending to be her own mother, with Louisa as her daughter. Meanwhile, the faithless Wildlove is exposed as Louisa's secret husband. In the resorting of relationships at the end, the Carrols are reconciled in matrimony, and Louisa is restored to her husband, Wildlove.

Play	First Produced	First Published

ANIMAL MAGNETISM   1788   N.D. 1788?
  First published in a pirated edition in Dublin

        Set in France in the house of a quack doctor,
this three-act farce, first presented at Covent
Garden, introduces the doctor's young ward,
Constance, whom he is set on marrying himself
against her will, and her lively and resourceful
maid and confidante, Lisette. Constance, though
strictly confined to the house, has fallen in love
with a young man, the Marquis de Lancy, who with
his quick-witted servant, LaFleur, haunts the
street below her window. The quack doctor has
failed to gain the recognition he has sought from
the medical authorities, and so adopts a new cult
practice called Animal Magnetism. LaFleur gains
access to his house by posing as the cult's
representative; this enables him to act as
go-between for Constance and the Marquis. Lisette
proves a very willing party to the deception.
LaFleur gives the doctor one of the cult's magic
wands, and he is gulled into believing that animal
magnetism can be used to induce Constance to fall
in love with him. Immediately the 'magic' appears
to get out of hand - both Constance and Lisette
pretend violent love for the doctor to his growing
embarrassment; indeed, the whole household appears
to be going mad through the erotic effects of the
wand. The Marquis himself is first introduced by
LaFleur as a demonstration patient; then LaFleur
feigns death, seemingly as a result of the doctor's
misuse of the wand. The Marquis, posing next as
another healer, rescues the doctor from his
terrible dilemma and, revealing his true identity,
claims Constance as his reward. Love then emerges
as the only reliable and natural form of animal
magnetism.

THE CHILD OF NATURE   1788   1788

        A play in two acts presented in Covent Garden
and set in Spain, The Child of Nature was another
of Elizabeth Inchbald's adaptations from the French
- Zélie, by Madame the Marchioness of Sillery. The
seventeen-year-old Amanthis has been so confined by
her middle-aged guardian, the Marquis Almanza, that
she is totally ignorant of the world. The Marquis
is in love with this seemingly penniless girl - a

match opposed by his elderly guardian. His rival is the libertine Count Valentia. Things end happily when the girl's father turns up to reveal her gentle birth and potential wealth, making her after all a suitable match for the Marquis, while Valentia is claimed by a wealthy Marchioness he has also been courting.

THE MARRIED MAN	1789	1789

First presented at the Little Theatre, Haymarket, The Married Man is a comedy in three acts adapted from Philippe-Néricault Destouches' sentimental play, Le Mari, houteux de l'être, on La Philosophe marié. The studious Sir John Classick finds his recent, secret marriage to a young wife, Matilda, disturbs his studies; his friend, Dorimant, who had advised him to marry, aims to wed Matilda's sister, Emily. Matilda pleads with her husband to make their marriage public since the libertine Lord Lovemore, thinking her single, is trying to pay her court, while Emily is becoming jealous because of this. Sir John, too, is jealous because of Lord Lovemore's attentions to his wife. All is therefore set for a comedy of prolonged misunderstanding, complicated by the threat of Sir John's rich uncle that he will disinherit him if he does not marry an heiress of his choice.

THE HUE AND CRY	1791	Not published

A farce in two acts, presented at Drury Lane, and set in Madrid. Don Lewis has an unnamed, prospective husband for his daughter, Leonora, who has meanwhile become attracted by a stranger she has met at a carnival, Count Abbeville of France. This same man is forced to take refuge in Don Lewis's house when pursued by the police for the alleged killing of Leonora's jealous cousin, Don Juan, who had challenged the Count to a duel after seeing the attentions he was paying to Leonora at the carnival. Abbeville is concealed from all, including Don Lewis, by Leonora's contriving maid, Iris; he is unaware he is in fact Leonora's prospective husband; all he knows is that he has fallen in love with the lady he met at the carnival. Iris spirits Abbeville and his servant Perroquet away concealed in chests, but meanwhile the police have arrested Don Juan and his servant for allegedly killing <u>his</u> opponent. Finally, all four men meet in prison, and a happy end becomes automatic since nobody has, after all, killed anybody, while Abbeville is in any case the intended husband of the very girl he loves.

NEXT DOOR NEIGHBOURS 1791   1791

This comedy was presented at the Theatre Royal, Haymarket; it was partially adapted from <u>L'Indigent</u> of L.S. Mercier and <u>Le Dissipateur</u> of Destouches, and is in three acts set in London. Bluntly, the honest agent of the spendthrift Sir George Splendorville, discovers a poverty-stricken brother and sister, Harry and Eleanor, starving in a rented room in the house next door owned by a corrupt lawyer, Blackman. Prompted by Bluntly, Sir George offers financial help to the couple and their father, confined in a debtors' prison, provided he is given access to Eleanor. As a result, the beautiful Eleanor finds Sir George only too anxious to press his attentions on her. Blackman succeeds in his efforts to get into Sir George's service, a position strengthened when Sir George suddenly loses his fortune at play to his wealthy female counterpart, Lady Caroline Seymour. Blackman's schemes to secure a potential fortune for Sir George are frustrated when Eleanor is revealed by an honest lawyer to be the true inheritor. Sir George is saved by marriage to Lady Caroline, and Eleanor marries the man previously thought to be her brother, but in reality not so.

THE MASSACRE   Never staged; published in
                      Boaden's <u>Memoirs of Mrs.</u>
                      <u>Inchbald</u>, 1833

The play was type-set for publication, but withdrawn by Mrs. Inchbald; it is subtitled, 'Taken from the French,' but with no further indication as to its source. The scene is set in a small French town some sixty miles from Paris at the time of the persecution of the Protestants and the Massacre of St. Bartholomew's Day (1572). Friends gather round Mme. Tricastin, whose husband, Eusebat, is an active resistance agent among the Protestants. He arrives from Paris, where he reveals an 'infernal massacre' is taking place, and describes its horror. They persuade him, against his will, to take flight with them to England, leaving in separate groups. But a price has been set on Tricastin's head, and they are confronted by a hostile mob; Tricastin's father tries to pose as his son, but only Mme. Tricastin manages to escape with their children. At a summary trial, Eusebat is condemned: 'His crime: not to think with us.' A counter-revolutionary mob of soldiers intervenes to save him, but bearing the slaughtered body of Mme. Tricastin and the children.

YOUNG MEN AND OLD WOMEN 1792   Not published

Presented at the Little Theatre, Haymarket, this two-act farce was adapted from J.B. Gresset's Le Méchant (1747), and is preserved in the Larpent Collection at the Huntington Library, listed as of unknown authorship. (According to Prof. Allardyce Nicoll, A History of the English Drama 1660-1900, pp. 275, 334, 388 of Vol. III, Late Eighteenth Century Drama, this manuscript is Elizabeth Inchbald's play listed under the alternative title, Lovers no Conjurers, and with no author credited.) Knaveston, who is in love with his neighbor, Sir Samuel Prejudice's daughter, Lydia, is dismayed by the unexpected arrival of his friend Sylvan, from overseas. Sylvan is due to marry Lydia (whom he has not met) or forfeit his inheritance as a result of the long-arranged marriage settlement established between his father, recently dead, and Sir Samuel. Knaveston tries to put his friend off the marriage by representing Lydia as a fickle flirt, and suggesting that he behaves badly when he visits Sir Samuel so that he, the father, will want to abandon the marriage agreement, and so enable Sylvan to keep his inheritance. Once in Sir Samuel's house, however, Sylvan regrets his assumed boorish behavior, since he finds Lydia very attractive. He tries, at first unsuccessfully, to make amends, while Knaveston takes advantage of the situation to press his own suit. All ends happily, though complicated for a while further by the absurd comic behavior of Sir Samuel's widowed sister, Mrs. Ambiology, who is in the habit of inventing and repeating falsehoods, though seemingly only too anxious to correct her ways.

Play	First Produced	First Published

EVERYONE HAS HIS FAULT 1793   1793

An original comedy in five acts set in London, and
presented at Covent Garden. Well supplied with
peripheral comic characters, like Mr. Solus who
does not know whether he wants to marry or no, and
Mr. and Mrs. Placid who enjoy being perpetually at
loggerheads, the central action has two interwoven
strands. First, that of Irwin and his run-away
wife, Lady Eleanor (disinherited by her father,
Lord Norland), who have returned to London after a
long spell abroad and are living in dire poverty;
they had to abandon their son when they left
England, and from their point of view this son,
though now grown up, is lost to them. Second,
there is Sir Robert Ramble (the play's best and
most complex character), who has just divorced his
wife, a ward of Lord Norland, after a brief
marriage during which he neglected her. He is
suffering increasing remorse, while Lord Norland's
one desire is to get his ward, known now as Miss
Woburn, remarried. Busy throughout the play is the
kindly Mr. Harmony, who is anxious to help
everyone. The happy end is contrived very happily;
Sir George is reconciled with his former wife, and
Lady Eleanor's lost son is discovered to be a
renamed ward of Lord Norland, who is reconciled
with his daughter.

THE WEDDING DAY   1794   1794

An original short drama in two acts presented at
Drury Lane. Sir Adam Contest's absentee,
middle-aged son, Tom, returns from abroad on the
very day the elderly Sir Adam is marrying an
eighteen-year old bride, to whom he cannot refrain
from boasting about the virtues of his former wife
(thought to be dead). The bride symbolically loses
her wedding-ring after the ceremony. Tom's
libertine friend, Lord Rakeland, loses no time
making advances to the new Lady Contest, while Tom
makes it clear that he wants to marry a lady (Lady
Autumn) he has met abroad and who has also recently
returned to London with a mysterious person, Mrs.
Hamford, who had been living away from England for
twelve years. Mrs. Hamford turns out to be Sir
Adam's previous wife, making his new marriage
null-and-void, while the youthful ex-bride turns out

to be Lady Autumn's daughter. So Tom Contest turns
from stepson to uncle when he marries Lady Autumn,
and the ex-bride is liberated to enjoy her new
freedom in London society.

WIVES AS THEY WERE AND
MAIDS AS THEY ARE   1797   1797

An original comedy in five acts set primarily in
London and presented at Covent Garden. In her
introduction to this play, Elizabeth Inchbald
specifically links the heroine of A Simple Story,
Miss Milner, with the heroine of this play, Maria
Dorrillon. Miss Milner is commonly interpreted as
having some at least of the characteristics of
Elizabeth herself.

The comedy turns on concealed identity
maintained until near the end of the play, though
known to the audience from the very start. Maria,
daughter of Sir William Dorrillon, has been the
ward of the kindly but weak Mr. Norberry during her
father's prolonged absence abroad. She has never
seen her father, and now that he has returned he
persuades Norberry to introduce him to her as plain
Mr. Mandred. Mandred cannot refrain from fatherly
reproof of Maria concerning her great extravagance
and even more that of her companion, Lady Raffle;
Maria has two unwanted suitors, Sir George Evelyn
and Mr. Bronzely. Another wing of the action
concerns a friend of Norberry, Lord Priory and his
exaggeratedly compliant wife, whom he has until now
kept in seclusion from the corrupt influences of
London society. She is, however, much attracted by
Bronzely, who has given her an accidental kiss, and
she consents to elope with him to the as-yet
unoccupied house Lord Priory is preparing for their
occupation in London; once there, however, she
occupies herself with continual knitting to
Bronzely's frustration. Meanwhile, Maria and Lady
Raffle, who has run up large gaming bills, are
arrested for debt, and Sir William (Mandred) is
forced to bail them out. In the end, Lady Priory
returns intact to her 'reformed' husband, Maria has
her beloved father and a future husband in Sir
George, while Lady Raffle gladly accepts Bronzely
rather than have no husband at all.

Play	First Produced	First Published
LOVERS' VOWS	1798	1798

This five-act play, adapted from A.F. von Kotzebue's Child of Love, is set in Germany. It was presented at Covent Garden. The poverty-stricken Agatha comes across her long-lost, illegitimate son, Frederick (a soldier seeking his discharge) while she is begging in the streets; they join forces and are housed by kindly villagers. As Agatha's story emerges, she is shocked to learn that her seducer is the local landowner, Baron Wildenheim, now a widower with a daughter, Amelia, who is secretly in love with her tutor, Anhalt, an ordained man and spiritual adviser to her father, who has become deeply repentant concerning his past life. The Baron demands that Anhalt counsel Agatha about love and marriage, which leads to amusing scenes of double entendre as they inevitably discover their love for each other. Meanwhile, Frederick, begging on behalf of his mother, openly threatens the Baron when he offers him only a trifle. The Baron orders his immediate arrest. Amelia pleads for the young prisoner, and when his true identity as the Baron's illegitimate son is revealed, the Baron makes amends by marrying Agatha, and allowing his daughter to marry her lover, Anhalt.

THE WISE MAN OF THE EAST	1799	1799

A comedy in five acts presented at Covent Garden; adapted from Kotzebue, and set in London. Claransforth is determined to enjoy life now that his rich father reportedly has died in India, leaving him a fortune. The family's financial adviser, Bankwell, pleads with Claransforth to help an old friend of his father, Metland, who has become impoverished after placing his fortune of 12,000 pounds in the elder Claransforth's hands, without receipt and lost it when Claransforth's home abroad was burnt to the ground. Bankwell also introduces to the younger Claransforth a Wise Man from the East called Ava Thoanoa, another contact with his father. This Wise Man claims he knows all about Claransforth's way of life and of his intentions to seduce Ellen, Metland's daughter, now waiting maid to the worldly Lady Mary Diamond, much to her father's disapproval. Lady Mary exploits

Ellen's beauty to attract young spendthrifts to her
pharo-table, among them Claransforth. Another
family, Starch, who are quakers, have a daughter,
Ruth, who is in love with Metland's son, a young
Ensign. Ellen warns Claransforth of the loaded
dice used by Lady Mary, but Claransforth, offering
to take her home, actually abducts her and takes
her to a house of vice. Metland, at the moment his
furniture is being taken by the bailiffs, discovers
his 12,000 pounds in a secret drawer in a desk
given him by the elder Claransforth. Ellen escapes
from Claransforth's clutches, and the latter, sorry
for what he did on impulse, places him in Ava
Thoanoa's hands. A reformed Claransforth is able
to marry Ellen, and Ruth marries her Ensign. Ava
Thoanoa turns out to be Claransforth the Elder,
alive and well in his Eastern disguise.

A CASE OF CONSCIENCE   Written 1800-01 for John
                              Philip Kemble and Sarah
                              Siddons, but never
                              presented; published
                              posthumously by Boaden in
                              his Memoirs of Mrs.
                              Inchbald (1933).

A drama in five acts set in Spain. The Marquis of
Romono's only son, Count Oviedo, has just returned
after three years military service, along with his
servant, Girone. Oviedo is disturbed to find the
Marquis estranged from his formerly much-loved
wife, Adriana, and opposed now to his son's
formerly agreed betrothal to his ward, Eudora. The
Marquis has discovered evidence that Oviedo is not
his son, but the child of Duke Cordunna, to whom
Adriana had been previously betrothed, deserting
him for the Marquis. Manuel, a priest who acts as
confidant to the whole family, is possessed of this
knowledge, and under the Marquis's orders takes
Eudora to a nunnery; a nearby hermit, known as
Salvador, is induced by the Marquis to test
Adriana's good faith, posing as a messenger from
Cordunna. However, he actually is Cordunna and
begs Adriana to elope with him, her former lover.
Meanwhile the overzealous Girone, thinking to help
his master, Count Oviedo, liberates Eudora by
force; this crime against sanctuary leads officers
of the Inquisition to arrest both Oviedo and Girone,

while Eudora takes secret refuge in Salvador's hermitage. Oviedo is reported to have died under torture, and the Marquis, though still convinced his absent wife is guilty, becomes stricken with remorse. Adriana refuses to go further with the elopement, while Cordunna is condemned by the Inquisition for impersonating a monk and is exposed as a victim of passion conspiring to steal the Marquis's wife. Manuel persuades the Inquisitors to release Oviedo, who is still alive and in the guise of an unknown challenger, pursues Cordunna and kills him in a duel. The Marquis accepts Adriana back as his wife, and recognizes Oviedo as his true son. Oviedo is betrothed once again to his love, Eudora.

TO MARRY OR NOT TO MARRY	1805	1805

A comedy in five acts set in England; presented at Covent Garden. Sir Oswin Mortland, a confirmed bachelor in his thirties, lives on his country estate with his widowed elder sister, Mrs. Sarah Mortland. The latter is surprised by the sudden arrival of a young girl she barely knows, Hester Ashdale, pleading for refuge; she has run away at the last moment to escape from an unwanted marriage. Sir Oswin reluctantly consents to let her stay, and also agrees to his uncle, Lord Danberry, arranging his marriage to Lady Susan Courtly. The jilted bridegroom turns out to be Sir Oswin's old schoolfriend, Willowear, who arrives in some agitation to claim back his fiancée. Sir Oswin manages to persuade him to seek another bride, suggesting that Lady Susan Courtly might well do, especially as he had once proposed to her in the past, as he has to many other women. Meanwhile Sir Oswin has become increasingly attracted by Hester with her down-to-earth views against marriage. Mrs. Mortland is warned not to let him know that Hester's family name is Lavensforth - a name deeply offensive to the Mortlands since a Lavensforth had some thirty years before threatened Sir Oswin's life when a child, and as a result had been judicially exiled. Lavensforth has served his term in exile and returned with his black servant, Amos, all the more anxious to assassinate Sir Oswin now that he is preventing his daughter, Hester's arranged marriage. Sir Oswin, now in love with Hester, is shocked nevertheless to discover she is Lavensforth's daughter, though there is now growing doubt Lavensforth did indeed threaten his life in the past. Amos does, however, manage to wound Sir Oswin when he is out with Hester, but the play ends in reconciliation; Hester is betrothed to Sir Oswin, and Willowear secures Lady Susan.

BIBLIOGRAPHY

I.   WORKS BY ELIZABETH INCHBALD
      Based   substantially   on   the   detailed
      bibliography compiled by G. Louis Joughin,
      and published by the University of Texas,
      Studies in English No. 14, 1934, and on the
      listings in Allardyce Nicoll's A History of
      English Drama, Vol. III, Late 18th Century
      Drama, pp. 275 and 388.

(i)   Books

      A Simple Story, 1791. Several reprints and
      revised   editions   supervised   by   Elizabeth
      Inchbald.   Principal   later   reprints   1810,
      1823, 1831, 1848, 1849, 1851, 1880, 1885,
      1908. 1967, 1977. Irish editions 1791,
      1804.   American   edition   (as   The Mourning
      Ring) 1822. French translation 1792, 1793,
      1808, 1833, 1834. German translation 1792.

      Nature   and   Art,   1796;   reprint   1797.
      Principal later reprints 1810, 1823, 1880,
      1886. American edition, Philadelphia 1796.
      Swiss-French   translation   1797.   French
      edition 1830. German translation, ND. (An
      abridged edition appeared in 1915 in Boston,
      USA in The English Novel before the 19th
      Century, Excerpts from Representative Types,
      selected by A. Hopkins and H. Hughes, pp.
      703-736.)

      The British Theatre, 1806-09. 25 volumes,
      with five plays in each volume, selected by
      the publisher, but edited with biographical
      and critical comment by Elizabeth Inchbald.
      An edition in 20 volumes with 100 plays
      appeared in 1824.

      Collection of Farces and Afterpieces, 1809.
      7   volumes.   Reprinted   1815.   Elizabeth
      Inchbald acted as selector only.

      The Modern Theatre, 1811. 10 volumes.
      Elizabeth Inchbald acted as selector only.

(ii) Plays

The following initials indicate that the play
was selected for inclusion in the
undermentioned collections:

The British Theatre, 1806-09. BT
Collection of Farces and Afterpieces, 1809. FA
The Modern Theatre, 1811. MT
The London Stage. London, 1834-37. LS
Cumberland's The British Theatre. London
1825-55. CBT
The British Drama. London, 1872. BD
Dicks' Standard Plays. London, 1833. DSP

* before a title indicates there is a
manuscript of the play in the Larpent
Collection at the Huntington Library, USA.

*A Mogul Tale (1784). Published 1796, 1824.
LS; CBT; DSP.
*I'll Tell You What (1785). Published 1786.
(German translation, 1792). MT.
*Appearance is Against Them (1785).
Published 1785, 1824. LS; DSP.
The Widow's Vow (1786). Published 1786.
*All on a Summer's Day (1787). Never
published.
*Such Things Are (1787). Published 1788; 13
editions by 1805. BT; LS; DSP.
*The Midnight Hour (1787). Published 1787,
1788. FA: LS: CBT; BD; DSP.
*Animal Magnetism (1788). Published 1789,
1792, 1824, 1827, 1829, 1834, 1858. LS; CBT;
BD; DSP.
The Child of Nature (1788). Published 1788,
1789, 1790, 1794, 1800. FA; LS; CBT; DSP.
*The Married Man (1789). Published 1789.
*The Hue and Cry (1791). Never published.
*Next Door Neighbours (1791). Published
1791. MT.
The Massacre (1792). Set by the printers but
never published, 1792. (A rare copy of this
unpublished edition is held by the Library of
Congress.) Finally published 1833 by Boaden
in his Memoirs of Mrs. Inchbald, Vol. I.
Young Men and Old Women (1792). Never
published. [Allardyce Nicoll, op.cit. p. 388
claims the script of the play survives in the
Larpent Collection with the title Lovers no

Conjurers, but without credit to any author..]
*Everyone has his Fault (1793). Published
1793; seven editions by 1805. BT; CBT; DSP.
[The only one of Elizabeth Inchbald's plays
to appear in a modern edition: included by
Allardyce Nicoll in his Oxford University
Press anthologies, English Comedies of the
18th Century (1926) and Lesser English
Comedies of the 18th Century (1927).]
*The Wedding Day (1794). Published 1794.
FA; LS; CBT; DSP.
*Wives as They Were and Maids as They Are
(1797). Published 1797; five editions in the
same year. BT; LS; CBT; DSP.
*Lovers' Vows (1798). Published 1798.
Eleven editions by 1799, published by
Robinson, and five editions by Longman by
1805. BT; LS; CBT; BD; DSP.
*The Wise Man of the East (1799). Published
1799, with two further editions the same
year. MT.
A Case of Conscience (1800). Published
posthumously bo Boaden, op.cit, Vol. II, 1833.
To Marry or not to Marry (1805). Published
1805. BT.

The following plays had Irish editions:

Animal Magnetism. Dublin, 1789 (?), 1792.
Appearance is Against Them. Dublin, 1786.
The Child of Nature. Dublin, 1789.
Everyone has his Fault. Dublin, 1793, 1795.
I'll Tell You What. Dublin, 1787.
Lovers' Vows. Dublin, 1798, 1806; Cork, 1799.
The Married Man. Dublin, 1789.
The Midnight Hour. Dublin, 1788.
Next Door Neighbours. Dublin, 1791.
Such Things Are. Dublin, 1788.
The Wedding Day. Dublin, 1795.
The Widow's Vow. Dublin, 1786.
The Wise Man of the East. Dublin, 1800.
Wives as They Were. Dublin, 1797; Cork, 1797?

The following plays had American editions:

Animal Magnetism. New York, 1809.
The Child of Nature. Philadelphia, 1790; New
York 1806.
Everyone has his Fault. Philadelphia, 1794,
1822, 1827; Boston, 1809.

Lovers' Vows. Boston, 1799; Philadelphia,
1829.
The Midnight Hour. Boston, 1795, 1823; New
York, 1811.
A Mogul Tale. New York, 1827; Philadelphia,
1841.
To Marry or not to Marry. Baltimore, 1805.
The Wedding Day. New York, 1819.
The Widow's Vow. New York, 1787.
Wives as They Were. New York, 1813, 1825.

II. GENERAL BOOK LIST

Allen, Walter.	The English Novel. London, Penguin Books, 1958.
Austen, Jane.	Mansfield Park. 1814.
Boaden, James.	Memoirs of the Life of John Philip Kemble, London, 1825. Memoirs of Mrs. Siddons, London, 1827. The Life of Mrs. Jordan. London, 1831. Memoirs of Mrs. Inchbald. London, 1833.
Brown, Ford K.	Life of William Godwin. London, J.M. Dent., 1926.
Campbell, Thomas.	Life of Mrs. Siddons. London, 1834.
Collins, A.S.	The Profession of Letters: a Study of the Relationship of Author to Patron, Publisher, Public 1780-1832. London, Routledge, 1928.
Defoe, Daniel.	A Tour through England and Wales, 1724-27. London, J.M. Dent, Everyman Library.
Fitzgerald, Percy.	The Kembles. London, 1871.
Genest, John.	Some Account of the English Stage from 1660-1830. Vol. VII. Bath, 1832.
Godwin, William.	Memoirs of Mary Wollstonecraft.

London, 1798. Reprint: London,
Constable Miscellany, 1928.

Caleb Williams. London, 1794.
Reprint. London, Oxford
English Novel Series, 1970.

Hartnoll, Phyllis. (editor) The Oxford Companion to the
Theatre. London, Oxford
University Press, 1952.

Hazlitt, William. Complete Works. London,
J.M. Dent, 1930-34.

Hogan, Chas.Beecher. The Theatrical Managers in
England and America. Edited by
Joseph W. Donohue. Princeton
University Press, 1971.
(Especially for Tate Wilkinson)

Holcroft, Thomas. Memoirs. Edited by William
Hazlitt. London, 1816.

Joughin, George L. The Life and Work of Elizabeth
Inchbald, 1933. Dissertation
in Harvard University Library.

An Inchbald Bibliography.
Reprinted from the University
of Texas Studies in English,
No. 14, 1934.

Kelly, Gary. The English Jacobin Novel,
1780-1805. London, Oxford
University Press, 1976.

Kelly, Linda. The Kemble Era: John Philip
Kemble, Sarah Siddons, and the
London Stage. New York, Random
House, 1980.

Kemble, Frances Ann. Record of a Girlhood. London,
1878.

Littlewood, Sam. R. Elizabeth Inchbald and her
Circle. London, Daniel
O'Connor, 1921.

Mander, Raymond, and
Mitchenson, Joe. The Theatres of London. London,

Rupert Hart-Davis, 1963.

A Picture History of the
British Theatre. London,
Hulton Press, 1957.

Manvell, Roger.   Sarah Siddons. London,
                       Heinemann, 1970.

Marshall, Peter H.   William Godwin. New Haven and
                       London, Yale University Press,
                       1984.

McKee, William.   Elizabeth Inchbald. Ph.D.
                       Thesis, Washington, 1935.

Nicoll, Allardyce.   A History of the English Drama
                       1660-1900: Vol. III, Late 18th
                       Century Drama. Cambridge
                       University Press, 1955.

                       Introduction to Lesser English
                       Comedies of the 18th Century.
                       Oxford University Press, 1927.
                       The volume contains Elizabeth
                       Inchbald's play, Everyone has
                       his Fault.

Nicolson, Harold.   The Age of Reason, London,
                       Constable and Co., 1960.

Park, B.R.   Thomas Holcroft and Elizabeth
                       Inchbald: Studies in the 18th
                       Century Drama of Ideas. Ph.D.
                       Thesis for the Faculty of
                       Philosophy, Columbia
                       University, 1952.

Paul, C. Kegan.   William Godwin: his Friends
                       and Contemporaries. New York,
                       AMS Press, 1970, reprinted from
                       the London edition of 1876.

Playfair, Giles.   The Prodigy: the Strange Life
                       of Master Betty. London,
                       Secker and Warburg, 1967.

Plumb, J.H.   England in the Eighteenth
                       Century. London, Penguin Books,
                       1950.

210

Rogers, Samuel.   Recollections of the Table Talk
                       of Samuel Rogers. 1856.
                       Edition: London, Richards
                       Press, 1952.

Rousseau,   Emile. Edition: Emile for
Jean-Jacques.   Today, Edited by William Boyd.
                       London, Heinemann Educational,
                       1956.

                       La Nouvelle Héloïse. Translated
                       by J.M. McDowell, Pennsylvania
                       State University, 1968.

Siddons,   The Reminiscences of Sarah
Sarah Kemble.   Kemble Siddons. Edited by
                       William Van Lennep. Cambridge,
                       Mass., Widener Library, 1942.

Southerne, Richard.   The Georgian Playhouse. London,
                       Pleiades Books, 1948.

Sunstein, Emily W.   A Different Face: Life of Mary
                       Wollstonecraft. New York,
                       Harper and Row, 1975.

Taylor, John.   Records of my Life. London.
                       1832.

Tobler, Clara.   Mrs. Elizabeth Inchbald.
                       (In German). 1910.

Tompkins, J.M.S.   Introduction to A Simple Story.
                       Oxford English Novels Series.
                       London, Oxford University
                       Press, 1967 (paperback, 1977).

                       The Popular Novel in England
                       1770-1800. London, 1961.

Wardle, Ralph M.   Collected Letters of Mary
                       Wollstonecraft. Cornel
                       University Press, 1979.

Wilkinson, Tate.   Memoirs of His Own Life.
                       Dublin, 1791. The Wandering
                       Patentee. York and London,
                       1795. Facsimile edition:
                       London, Scolar Press, 1973.

Wollstonecraft,   Mary, 1788.
Mary.   The Wrongs of Women, 1798.
                     Published together in one
                     volume by Oxford University
                     Press, London, 1976.

                     Vindication of the Rights of
                     Women, 1792. Reprint, London,
                     Pelican Books, 1975.
                     (See also under Sunstein, Emily
                     W. and Wardle, Ralph M.).

Woolf, Virginia.   Women and Fiction. Essay in
                     Granite and Rainbow. London,
                     Hogarth Press, 1958.

Wyndham, H.S.   The Annals of Covent Garden
                     Theatre from 1732 to 1897.
                     London, 1906.

INDEX

127; editor of The British Theatre, 127; her work
as commentator and critic, 127-145; later London
residences, 147; her final years, 147-164; later
financial circumstances, 148; writes and considers
publication of her memoirs, 149-151; orders their
destruction, 151; letters to Mrs. Phillips (her
literary executor) 152, 163; her self-description,
164; her diary, 185-186.

Elizabeth Inchbald, 66-68, 176; praised by Maria
     Edgeworth, 159-160
Simpson, Debbie (sister), 37
Simpson, Dolly (sister), 37
Simpson, Edward (brother), 151
Simpson, George (brother), 4, 37
Simpson, Mary (mother), 3, 8, 11
Slender, Mrs. (sister), 6, 11
Smollett, Tobias George, 8, 61, 65
Southerne, Thomas, 130, 140
Southey, Robert, 105
Spectator, The, 63, 138
St. Leon (Godwin), 43, 106
Staël, Anne-Louise-Germaine Necker, Mme. de,
     161-162, 183
Steele, Sir Richard, 63
Sterling, Mr. (actor), 13, 24
Sterne, Laurence, 61, 65
Stockdale (publisher), 66
Strictures on the Modern System of Female Education
     (More), 68
Such Things Are (1787, Inchbald), 47, 53, 54, 55,
     57, 58, 192
Suett, Dicky, 24, 26

Table Talk (Rogers), 163
Tate, Nahum, 138
Taylor, John, 42, 56, 150, 157
Tempest, The (Shakespeare), 3
Terence, 47
Texier, Mon le, 36
Theatres, legitimate and illegitimate, 9; training
     for, 10
Thrale, Henry and Hester, 8
To Marry or not to Marry (1805, Inchbald), 46, 49,
     52, 202
Tompkins, J.M.S., 72, 90
Treason Trials (1794), 108
True Briton, The, 38
Twiss, Francis, 33, 48

Unfortunate Traveller, The (Nash), 63

Vanbrugh, Sir John, 139
Vicar of Wakefield, The (Goldsmith), 65
Vindication of the Rights of Woman, A
     (Wollstonecraft), 68
Voltaire, François-Marie Arouet, 9

Walcot, Dr. John ('Peter Pindar'), 27, 171